The Elegant Economical EGG Cookbook

The Elegant Economical EGG Cookbook

BY LOU SEIBERT PAPPAS

Drawings by Marion Seawell

101 Productions
San Francisco

Published by 101 Productions
834 Mission Street
San Francisco, California 94103

Distributed to the book trade in the United States
by The Scribner Book Companies, New York

Contents

With love to a beloved sister, Janet Seibert McCracken,
An inspirer of many culinary achievements

Nature endowed the world with a miraculous culinary ingredient—the egg. Each is a marvel in package design. Elliptically shaped, the brittle shell encases a unique product. When broken open, the whole egg is useful as a total concept. It is also easily divisible into two halves, both capable of performing diverse results. It may well be the most miraculous and versatile ingredient to enter the kitchen.

Eggs evoke fond memories of my childhood: Egg hunts Easter mornings as we scrambled for foil-wrapped Dutch chocolate eggs, jelly bean eggs and hand-dipped purple, pink and marbelized eggs ... sugar-crusted panoramic eggs and bright-eyed German wooden bunnies toting egg baskets on the dining room sideboard ... the ultra-fresh taste of just-laid brown eggs at Aunt Hilda's sheep ranch in Oregon ... special daily breakfasts at home and Mother's exclamation, ''Without an egg, you're not fit for school'' ... the tiny blue robin eggs in a nest tucked under an eave ... the race to lick the

dasher of the exquisite egg custard ice cream, churned every Sunday after Dad chopped the big ice block ...

Eggs elicit more recent memories: Yaya's Athenian avgolemono soup laden with poached chicken strips and plumped rice ... hot sausage slices and coddled eggs in a bitter greens salad at a charming Left Bank bistro ... ethereal egg puffs in a tiny Salzberg café and deciphering the equation from the non-bilingual chef ... scarlet eggs adorning the dove-shaped Italian Easter breads in Milan and Rome ... free-form, fish-shaped pirogs encasing chopped eggs, salmon and mushrooms in the artistic city of Helsinki! ... the dazzling smörgåsbord table at the Operakalleren in Stockholm with its bounty of egg choices ... stunning buttercream pastries at the fashionable Café Luitpold in Munich and a lesson in making baumkuchen by the handsome young pastry cooks ... the creamy frozen Italian mousses in a spectrum of flavors from Perché No's in Florence ...

—Lou Seibert Pappas
Portola Valley
April 17, 1976

Which Came First?

Which Came First?

The mythology, beliefs and customs surrounding the egg from ancient times to the present offer a fascinating tale. Legends of many pre-Christian peoples claimed that the world itself was created from an egg. Sanskrit verses in the Rig Veda sang of a cosmic egg with a spirit inside that would be born, die and be reborn. Egyptians believed that Ptah was the father of beginnings and creator of the egg of the sun and moon; an ancient drawing shows him at the potter's wheel turning out a golden egg. Phoenicians thought the egg was formed in primeval waters and split open to form two parts—heaven and earth.

Ancient peoples all over the world have ascribed magical powers to the egg. The Mayans relied on it to free persons thought to be under the spell of the ''evil eye''; medicine men handed an egg back and forth in front of the face of the bewitched. Gypsies buried eggs on river banks to avert floods. Moroccan children, who accidently stumbled into a stream, broke the supposed evil spell by throwing in an egg. The sorcerers of Rome told Nero's happy consort, Livia, that she would know the sex of her coming baby if she warmed an egg in her bosom until it hatched. A male chick emerged and Livia had a son, starting quite a fashion among the Roman ladies of that time.

Eggs were believed to insure fertility. German and Slav peasants smeared their ploughs with eggs and French brides used to break an egg on the threshold when entering the new home. These legends and customs have carried over into our age. In particular, the association of eggs with fertility and rebirth is reflected in Christian Easter customs, where the egg assumes resurrection significance. Even the time of Easter is appropriate—spring.

Which Came First?

All the world's egg festivals have a direct lineage from ancient times when the spirits of growth and fertility had to be encouraged or appeased. Many of the pagan egg ceremonies, from new year to midsummer, have been Christianized. Such ancient customs as the ceremonial breaking of eggs and the association of eggs with the color scarlet have carried into the present. Greeks form a circle and tap scarlet eggs end-to-end at Easter. The one finishing with an uncracked egg is destined to have good luck. Weddings in Morocco, Persia and Java are accompanied with the breaking of eggs.

Scarlet is the preferred egg color in many lands. Centuries before Christ, the Chinese marked the coming of spring with exchanges of scarlet eggs. In some Eastern European countries red eggs are brought to Easter midnight mass for blessing and eating. The Romanians exchange red eggs at Easter, believing they have potent charms. A Romanian legend explains that Mary, mother of Jesus, brought a basket of eggs to the soldiers who were guarding Mount Calvary in hopes of arousing their pity for Jesus' suffering. They ignored the gift, laid it beneath the cross, and as time passed, Christ's blood dripped down, coloring the eggs scarlet. (A similar Polish legend relates how the Virgin Mary brought a basket of eggs to Pontius Pilate, hoping he would intervene and save Jesus. She was too late, and when she saw Christ on the cross, she fainted, dropping the basket. The eggs rolled to the far corners of the earth.)

Children have long enjoyed the tradition of colored Easter eggs. The first written mention of "egg rolling" in Britain is in a Latin treatise of 1684. This sport is still a popular Easter pastime in England and Scotland. The eggs are rolled on grassy slopes, often a traditional hill, and the last child to have his egg break wins the roll. "Jollyboying" is another English custom. Children dress in costumes and go from house to house asking for eggs, similar to the Halloween custom in the United States. Swiss children receive eggs from the Easter cuckoo, but in other parts of Europe it is the prolific hare, a symbol of fertility, that leaves the eggs.

Beautifully decorated eggs predate Christianity by thousands of years and are especially associated with Russia and other Slavic countries. The peasants used a stylus, beeswax and brightly colored native dyes to fashion the renowned Ukrainian eggs. During the reign of Czar Nicholas II, this folk art blossomed. The court jeweler, Carl Fabergé, was commissioned to create imperial gifts for the Czar's family and friends. He turned out eggs in gold, platinum, enamel and precious gems. The jeweled eggs opened, containing intricate worlds inside, displaying exquisite workmanship and precision.

Contemporary Use

Man discovered very early that the egg was good to eat. We do not know precisely when the discovery was made, but an inscription of around 1450 B.C. says that Tutmoses III, on his Babylonian excursion, received as tribute four birds which laid eggs every day. Today the egg is used in countless ways in cuisines all over the world.

Which Came First?

Their decorative pirogs and culibiacs have an egg pastry encasing such things as chopped eggs with salmon, chicken, steak, mushrooms or green onions. Eggs enhance the babas, poppy seed cakes and the fruit-filled krendel, the traditional birthday coffee cake offered at breakfast.

The Scandinavians utilize eggs in many ways on their stunning buffet tables. There may be raw egg yolks tucked in steak tartare, omelets encasing sautéed mushrooms, lox and hard-cooked eggs trimmed with caviar. Cloudberry parfaits, mazarin tarts and buttery spritz cookies are golden with eggs.

The Japanese use eggs for steamed custards, tempura batter and dipping sauce for sukiyaki. A Chinese specialty called "thousand year eggs" involves curing eggs in lime for about six weeks. This gives them a grayish color, suggesting antiquity.

Indonesians adorn a rice table with hard-cooked eggs. The Parsis of the Gujarat State of India prepare a unique version of scrambled eggs, to which chiles, green peppers, onions or coriander are added, seasoned with curry spices.

In Mexico, huevos rancheros is a breakfast favorite—a delicious combination of fried eggs, tortillas and red chile sauce. The famous Latin American custard, flan, is made from milk, eggs, sugar and vanilla, caramelized much like the classic crème caramel of France.

And we must not ignore such American specialties as lemon angel pie, pecan pie, chiffon cake, and Caesar salad tossed with a raw egg.

The Italians conceal eggs in vegetable pies and frittatas, adorn mixed salads with egg slices, dip vegetable fritters in an egg coating and crank out tender egg pastas. They whip egg yolks to a froth in zabaglione, turn out egg-rich ice creams, mousses and spumones and produce ethereal dolci from a sponge-cake base adorned with chocolate curls, praline and buttercream.

The Greek cuisine is notable for its tangy avgolemono, the golden sauce of eggs and lemon that threads its way through varied savory dishes. It goes into the Easter soup and special sauces to bind meat, fish and chicken stews with vegetables. An almond soufflé sandwiched between crispy fila pastry is renowned among Greek sweets.

The Moroccan bastilla illustrates a fanciful egg pastry enclosing curried scrambled eggs, squab, and toasted almonds between crispy fila, showered with cinnamon-sugar.

The French have a knack with omelets, crêpes, soufflés and quiches, which appear in infinite variation in every course of the day, except at breakfast, where one rarely sees an egg unless specifically requested. And then there are the classic French sauces—béarnaise, hollandaise, mousseline.

The Spanish rely heavily on eggs for their omelets and lovely sponge cake desserts. The Portuguese tuck hard-cooked eggs in golden breads and produce a range of egg puff pastries filled with egg yolk and almond or citrus fillings.

The Russians celebrate Easter with a pyramid-shaped cheese mold called pashka and a stately bread named kulich, both laden with egg yolks.

The Egg Itself

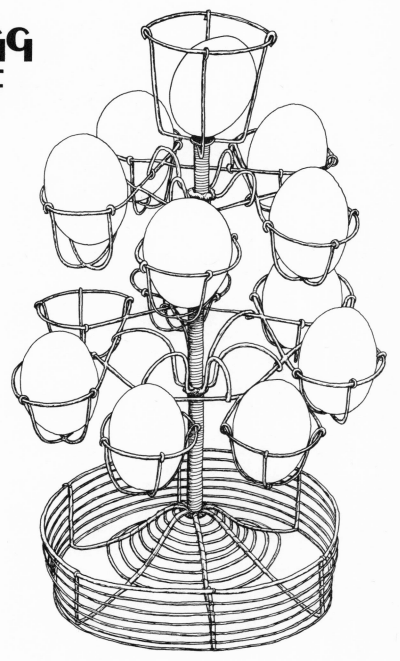

An egg is nature's most nearly perfect food, and its nutritive value is high. One large egg (about two ounces) contains 90 calories. Roughly, it is 10 percent shell, 60 percent white and 30 percent yolk. Of this the white is 90 percent water and 10 percent protein; the yolk is about 50 percent water, 17 percent protein and 33 percent fat. One large egg contains 6.8 grams protein, 7 grams fat, 32 milligrams calcium, 1.4 milligrams iron and vitamins A, D and riboflavin.

Eggs are graded according to quality and freshness. The three United States consumer grades for shell eggs are AA or Fancy Fresh, Grade A and Grade B. Grade AA, the highest quality table egg, and Grade A are the most desirable grades for eating simply as eggs—in the shell, poached, fried, or baked—because they have the freshest flavor and the yolks will stay well rounded and well centered. Grade B, an economical buy, is most suitable for general cooking and baking.

Candling is the commercial method of determining the interior quality on which egg grades are based. The process consists of holding and examining an egg against an electric light bulb in a dark room. This reveals the condition of the egg's interior. Defects on the yolk and foreign material on the white are easily seen. The size and shape of the yolk and the size of the air cell are noted. Originally this was done by candle, hence the name.

Eggs are sold by size as well as by grade. There is a difference of three ounces per dozen between each size. Jumbo is the largest, with one dozen weighing a minimum of 30 ounces. The other sizes in decreasing order are extra large, 27 ounces minimum for one dozen; large, 24 ounces; medium, 21 ounces; small, 18 ounces; and peewee, 15 ounces. Large size, or two-ounce eggs, are the right size to use for recipes in this book. It is the accepted size for all recipes in most cookbooks.

The Egg Itself

The Shell
The color of the shell varies from white to brown, depending upon the breed of the hen. The shell color does not affect the flavor, nutritive value or cooking performance of the egg, nor is it a dependable guide to yolk color.

The White
Fresh egg white has an opalescent appearance, and when the egg is broken onto a flat surface the white next to the yolk is thick and viscous and tends to hold its shape, while that on the outer edge is less viscous and thinner. As eggs age, hastened by keeping them in too warm an environment, the thick white tends to become thin.

The Yolk
The yolk is anchored near the center of the egg by a dense cordlike strand of white called the chalaza, so that the yolk can revolve on its axis. The color of the yolk can range from light yellow to gold, depending on what the hen has been eating. The yolk in a fresh egg is round and upstanding. It is separated from the white by a membrane. As the egg deteriorates in quality, the yolk absorbs water from the white, swells and tends to flatten. Finally a stage is reached at which the yolk breaks through the separating membrane and the two portions combine.

On the surface of the yolk, a small light spot, called the "germ spot" may be seen. When an egg has been fertilized, the germ develops at this point. As the yolk swings in its hammock made by the chalaza, the gravity holds the yolk so that the germ spot is always on top—a plan of nature whereby it is always nearest the body of the hen as she sits on her eggs. For the production of market eggs, male birds are usually separated from the rest of the flock in order that infertile eggs may be produced. Infertile eggs keep better than fertile eggs. A red dot or spot on an egg signifies fertilization. You may remove it and still use the egg.

Freshness and Storage
As an egg ages, it becomes more alkaline and develops hydrogen sulfide, a compound of disagreeable odor that smells like some mineral waters. Overly long cooking or high temperature encourages the development of this odor and flavor even in a freshly laid egg. When you overcook a hard-cooked egg, the sulfur in the white combines with the iron in the yolk to form ferrous sulfide, a grayish-green ring surrounding the yolk.

To preserve freshness, store eggs in the refrigerator in their carton just as they are packed. This means the blunt end is up and the yolk stays centered. Do not place them near any strong-flavored foods since their shells are porous. Plan to use them within 10 to 14 days.

Egg whites may be stored in a covered jar in the refrigerator up to four days. They also freeze well; thaw and use them exactly as you would fresh egg whites. Egg yolks will also freeze but they do not soften completely when thawed; to use them in a blender-style mayonnaise or hollandaise, let thaw, then beat in the blender with a fresh yolk and proceed from there. Store raw yolks in a container and cover with a thin layer of cold water. This prevents the yolk from forming a hard skin. Refrigerate and use within four days. Refrigerate hard-cooked eggs up to four or five days.

Dried Eggs and Egg Substitutes

Dried eggs are available as dried whole eggs, egg yolks and egg whites. They are especially convenient for campers and backpackers. The equivalents of dried eggs to fresh eggs are: one whole fresh egg equals two tablespoons dried egg plus two and one-half tablespoons water; one fresh yolk equals one and one-half tablespoons dried yolk plus one tablespoon water; and one fresh white equals one tablespoon dried white plus two tablespoons water.

Low-cholesterol egg substitutes are also available in the marketplace. They are suited for use in any dish where the whole egg is beaten and blended in, such as crêpes, quiches, custards and frittatas.

PRINCIPLES OF EGG COOKERY

Besides being highly nutritious and enhancing the flavor and color of dishes, eggs perform at least six different cookery functions: thickening, leavening, emulsifying, binding, coating and clarifying. The actions are due to various qualities of the egg, but most of them happen because the protein of eggs, which is largely albumin and globulin, coagulates under heat.

Thickening

The different egg proteins coagulate at different temperatures, resulting in thickening. Egg white becomes jelly-like at 140° and firms at about 149°. Egg yolk coagulates around 144° and completes the process at 158°. A whole beaten egg coagulates at around 156°. The addition of other ingredients raises the coagulation temperature. Regardless of what the egg is mixed with, 190° is about the highest temperature it can reach without coagulating. When the egg coagulates, it first forms a clot, like a lacy network. If overheating occurs, the network contracts, forcing out the liquid. This explains why it is so important not to overcook egg dishes. The presence of a high amount of acid in an egg dish, such as a sauce or custard, will create a greater tendency for the mixture to curdle because the firming or coagulating action is quickened by the presence of an acid.

Leavening

The egg as a leavening agent is dependent upon the amount of air beaten into it and retained during its preparation. Its foaming capacity is used in making soufflés, sabayon sauce and cakes, such as angel or sponge. Egg white is more often used as a leavening agent than the yolk or whole egg because it forms a greater, more stable foam. When heat is applied, the air bubbles expand, the egg white stretches and then sets or coagulates, giving a light porous structure to the product.

Several factors affect the volume and stability of foams. Egg whites at room temperature foam

The Egg Itself

more rapidly and to a greater volume than those at refrigerator temperature. Salt and acids stabilize the foam since these substances cause proteins in the foam to coagulate slightly and give it strength. Sugar increases the strength of the foam so less air is lost in mixing. Any fat, such as an oily film on the bowl or a speck of yolk in the whites, decreases their ability to foam. It is important to not over-beat egg whites to the point where they are dry, stiff and brittle. Then they have expanded so much that they cannot stretch further during baking, and when air in them expands in the oven, the cell walls break and the structure collapses.

Emulsifying
Eggs act as an emulsifying agent because they can form a thin stable film around tiny globules of oil, as in mayonnaise. Egg yolk is a more efficient emulsifying agent than whole egg. Whole egg, in turn, is more efficient than egg white.

Binding
Eggs serve as binding agents, giving tenacity to cream puffs and popovers, letting them stretch and expand and still retain the leavening so they are light and well formed.

Coating
Eggs are used to coat foods, facilitating the adhesion of crumbs, flour, etc., and assisting in a nicely browned crust when cooked.

Clarifying
Egg white is useful in clarifying stock because as it coagulates it encloses within its meshes any foreign particles. Allowing two egg whites for each quart of stock, whip whites into cold stock and bring to a boil, beating with a wire whisk. Simmer 15 minutes and strain.

TECHNIQUES OF EGG COOKERY

Separating and Beating Eggs
Eggs separate more easily into yolks and whites when they are chilled. To separate eggs, crack the shell with a single brisk tap at its middle and with thumbs pull the shell apart. Let the white run out into a bowl and pass the yolk from shell to shell until it is completely free of white, taking care not to break the yolk on the sharp edge of the shell. Place the yolk in a bowl and transfer the white to a larger bowl. Repeat, always placing the new white in a small bowl by itself. If any trace of yolk should go in with the white, plan to use this white for scrambled eggs or another purpose. In this way you do not run the chance of contaminating your entire bowl of egg whites with a bit of yolk.

The yolk contains fat which prevents a good foam. The fat emulsifies the water in the egg whites, softens the proteins and weighs the whites down. As a result there is little foaming and very little increase in volume. Also, a film of water on the inside of a metal bowl prevents the development of static electricity between beaters and bowl, which is an asset to increasing foam. If your egg whites refuse to beat up properly, chances are the bowl or beaters were greasy and your only salvation is to start again with fresh egg whites and clean bowl and beaters. Therefore, always start with a clean dry bowl.

The bowl for beating egg whites should be stainless steel, tinned metal or hammered copper. Porcelain and glass bowls allow the beaten whites to fall down their slippery sides and lose volume; aluminum bowls will gray the eggs; and plastic bowls, in spite of careful washing, may retain an oily film deterring the increase in volume. It is important that the entire mass of egg whites be in motion at once; therefore the bowl should not be too wide and it should have a rounded bottom. If beating only one egg white, one yolk or one whole egg, use the smallest bowl that the beater will accommodate. Remember that egg whites mount to seven or eight times their original volume, so choose bowl size accordingly.

When beating egg yolks and sugar, some recipes say to beat until thick and lemon colored, or until they form a ribbon. This means that when the beating stops, the mixture should fall from the beater into the bowl in a long flat band that folds upon itself as a silk ribbon would do if laid down.

When making a stirred or baked custard, beat eggs just until blended, not foamy, so you do not have bubbles in the final product.

Folding
When folding egg whites into a batter or sauce as for a soufflé, it is wise to mix about one-fourth of the foam into the heavy batter to lighten it. Then put the remainder of the egg whites on top of the batter and with a rubber spatula, fold them in quickly. To fold, cut through whites and batter close to the center of the bowl down to the base and lift up the batter, turning it on top of the foam. Repeat, turning bowl.

Combining Yolks and Sauces
When making an egg yolk-thickened sauce, first beat yolks with a little cold liquid, then gradually incorporate the hot liquid so they are slowly heated. Or blend part of the hot sauce into the beaten yolks to warm them before stirring them into the remaining sauce. If these procedures are not followed, the eggs could curdle and turn granular. Once the yolks are incorporated into the sauce, the sauce may be brought to a boil if it is a flour-based sauce. Sauces without flour, such as avgolemono, should not be allowed to boil as the sauce will curdle.

Herbs
Parsley, chives, chervil and tarragon are frequently used to complement egg dishes. Other herbs that enhance omelets, scrambled eggs or soufflés are basil, dill, marjoram, oregano, summer savory and thyme. To substitute fresh herbs for dried herbs in a recipe, the ratio is three to one: One teaspoon dried herbs equals three teaspoons or one tablespoon fresh herbs.

Hors d'Oeufs

MINI-FRITTATA

Resembling a miniature quiche, *sans* crust, this hot appetizer may be filled with a variety of cooked vegetables, such as spinach, red or green peppers, zucchini squash or broccoli.

1 bunch green onions (approximately 6),
   finely chopped
4 tablespoons butter
1/4 pound mushrooms, sliced (approximately
   1 cup)
2 cloves garlic, minced
1/2 teaspoon crumbled dried tarragon
5 eggs
salt and pepper to taste
1/2 cup shredded Parmesan cheese

Using a large frying pan, sauté onions in 2 tablespoons of the butter until glazed. Add mushrooms and sauté 1 minute. Remove from heat and season with garlic and tarragon. Dot remaining butter in the bottom of 16 small muffin cups and heat the cups in a 425° oven. Beat eggs until blended and combine with sautéed vegetables, salt and pepper and 1/4 cup of the cheese. Spoon into the hot muffin cups and sprinkle tops with remaining cheese. Bake in a 425° oven for 8 to 10 minutes, or until set and puffed. Slip under the broiler to brown lightly. Let cool 1 minute, then remove from pans. Serve hot.
Makes 16 appetizers

GREEN ONION AND SPINACH FRITTATA

Cut this vegetable-strewn baked omelet in small squares or diamonds for an appetizer, or in large rectangles for a vegetable side dish.

4 bunches green onions (approximately 24),
   finely chopped
4 tablespoons butter
2 bunches spinach (approximately 2 pounds),
   finely chopped
6 tablespoons finely chopped parsley (or more,
   if desired)
12 eggs
1/2 cup sour cream or heavy cream
1-1/2 cups shredded Gruyère, Swiss or
   Cheddar cheese
3/4 cup shredded Parmesan cheese

Using a large frying pan, sauté onions in butter until glazed. Add spinach and sauté 2 minutes. Remove from heat, add parsley and set aside. Beat eggs until light and mix in sour cream, Gruyère cheese, half the Parmesan and the onion mixture. Pour into a well-buttered 10- by 15-inch jelly-roll pan. Sprinkle with remaining Parmesan cheese. Bake in a 350° oven for 25 minutes or until set. Cut in squares and serve hot.
Makes about 6 dozen appetizers,
or 10 to 12 side-dish servings

Hors d'Oeufs

PICKLED SPICED EGGS

Piquant spiced eggs are a choice accouterment to a picnic outing, along with sliced ham and other cold meats or a pâté.

16 hard-cooked eggs, cooled and shelled
1 quart white distilled vinegar
4 dried red chile peppers, seeded
1 tablespoon mixed pickling spices
1 teaspoon each black peppercorns, salt and
    mustard seeds

Pack eggs in 2 quart jars. Combine vinegar, peppers, pickling spices, peppercorns, salt and mustard seeds in a saucepan, bring to a boil and simmer uncovered for 15 minutes. Pour over eggs, seal, let cool and chill. Refrigerate for 2 days before using to allow flavors to permeate the eggs.
Makes 16 pickled eggs

PICKLED RED EGGS

Here is a novel accompaniment to cold meats, dark rye bread and dill pickles. Small cooked beets may also be pickled along with the eggs.

16 hard-cooked eggs, cooled and shelled
1 cup beet juice
3 cups cider vinegar
1 teaspoon each whole cloves, allspice and
    peppercorns
1/2-inch piece ginger root

Pack the eggs in 2 quart jars. Combine beet juice, vinegar and spices in a saucepan and simmer 10 minutes. Pour over eggs, seal, let cool and chill. Refrigerate a few days to allow flavors to permeate the eggs.
Makes 16 pickled eggs

CHINESE TEA EGGS

Tea eggs are certainly a conversation piece. When shelled they exhibit a beautiful marbelized appearance and an unusual spicy flavor. Serve them as a luncheon accompaniment.

8 eggs
3 tablespoons black tea
1/4 cup soy sauce
2 teaspoons aniseed

Place eggs in a saucepan and cover with water; simmer 10 minutes. Lift out of water and let cool slightly, reserving water. Tap the entire surface of each egg with the back of a spoon, making a fine crackled effect all over. Return eggs to the water and add tea, soy sauce, salt and aniseed. Cover and simmer 1 hour. Chill. Serve peeled and cut in quarters.
Makes 8 servings

CURRY-STUFFED EGGS

Sprightly Indian seasonings punctuate these stuffed eggs for a different appetizer.

1 clove garlic, minced
2 teaspoons curry powder
2 teaspoons butter
8 hard-cooked eggs
1 tablespoon Major Grey's chutney, chopped
3 tablespoons sour cream
2 tablespoons chopped roasted almonds or peanuts

Sauté the garlic and curry powder in butter for 2 or 3 minutes. Peel eggs and cut in half lengthwise. Mix curry seasonings with the egg yolks, chutney and sour cream, and return the yolk mixture to the egg whites. Sprinkle nuts over stuffed eggs.
Makes 16 appetizers

Hors d'Oeufs

HUNGARIAN HAM SQUARES

Smoky ham and sunflower seeds spark these egg squares for a high-protein appetizer.

6 eggs
3/4 cup sour cream or plain yogurt
1/2 teaspoon salt
1 cup finely chopped cooked ham
2 tablespoons each finely chopped parsley and
    green onion
1/2 cup shredded Swiss cheese
2 tablespoons butter, melted
1/4 cup hulled sunflower seeds
paprika

Beat eggs until light and mix in sour cream, salt, ham, parsley, onion, cheese, butter and 2 table-spoons of the seeds. Pour into a buttered 9-inch square pan. Sprinkle with remaining seeds and paprika. Bake in a 350° oven for 20 to 25 minutes or just until set. Cut in small squares and serve hot. (If desired, bake in advance and reheat in a 350° oven for 10 to 15 minutes, or until heated through.)
Makes about 2 dozen squares

TINY MUSHROOM PASTRIES

Cream cheese makes a flaky pastry for these bite-sized mushroom tarts.

1 small onion, finely chopped
2 tablespoons butter
1/2 pound mushrooms, chopped (approximately
    2 cups)
1/2 teaspoon salt
1/4 teaspoon each crumbled dried tarragon and
    freshly ground pepper
2 egg yolks
1/2 cup sour cream
Cream Cheese Pastry, page 25

Sauté onion in butter until golden. Add mushrooms and cook until glazed. Stir in salt, tarragon and pepper. Beat egg yolks and mix in sour cream. Add mushroom mixture and mix well. Line small 1-1/2-inch-to 2-inch tart pans with pastry by pressing a small ball of dough into pans, making it 3/16 inch thick. Spoon in filling until 3/4 full. Bake in a 400° oven for 20 to 25 minutes or until the pastry is golden brown.
Makes 2 to 3 dozen

FRENCH APPETIZER TART

This decorative first-course tart can have endless filling variations. Consider ripe olives, caviar and minced hard-cooked egg, or vary the pattern with shrimp or crab meat.

Savory Butter Crust, following
6 ounces cream cheese, at room temperature
4 tablespoons sour cream
salt and pepper to taste
dash Tabasco sauce
2 tablespoons chopped shallots
1 tablespoon chopped parsley
2 to 3 ounces sliced smoked salmon
3 hard-cooked eggs
2 green onions, chopped

Bake Savory Butter Crust as directed; cool. Beat cheese, sour cream, salt, pepper, Tabasco, shallots and parsley together until blended and spread in the baked tart shell. Cut salmon in small strips and arrange strips around the outer ring of the tart. Peel eggs, separate yolks and whites and finely chop whites and shred yolks. Make a ring of whites just inside salmon and follow with a ring of chopped onions and a circle of yolks in the center. Cover and chill until ready to serve.
Makes 10 first-course servings,
or 6 to 8 luncheon servings

SAVORY BUTTER CRUST

1 cup all-purpose flour
1 teaspoon grated lemon peel
1/4 pound butter
1 egg yolk

Place the flour, lemon peel and butter in a mixing bowl and mix until crumbly. Mix in the egg yolk and form into a ball. Pat dough onto the bottom and sides of an 11-inch fluted flan pan with removable bottom. Bake in a 425° oven for 8 to 10 minutes.
Makes 1 11-inch pastry crust

Hors d'Oeufs

EGGS WITH PESTO SAUCE

The fragrant Italian basil sauce makes a striking accompaniment to hard-cooked eggs for a first course, light lunch or picnic dish. If you like, add a few large cooked shrimp and cherry tomatoes to the platter.

1 cup lightly packed fresh basil leaves (if desired, substitute parsley for half the basil)
2 cloves garlic, minced
3 tablespoons pine nuts
2 walnut halves, chopped
1/3 cup freshly shredded Parmesan or Romano cheese
1/3 cup olive oil
1/4 teaspoon salt
6 hard-cooked eggs, halved lengthwise

Place in a blender container the basil, garlic, nuts, cheese, oil and salt. Blend until smooth. Turn into a small bowl and serve alongside the egg halves. Or if desired, arrange halves on a platter and spoon a little sauce over each egg.
Makes 6 servings

EGGS IN GREEN MAYONNAISE

A verdant green watercress mayonnaise coats softly cooked shelled eggs.

1 egg
1-1/2 tablespoons each freshly squeezed lemon juice and white wine vinegar
1/2 teaspoon salt
1 teaspoon Dijon-style mustard
1/4 teaspoon crumbled dried tarragon
2 tablespoons chopped parsley
1 shallot or green onion, chopped
1/4 cup each packed spinach and watercress leaves
1 cup safflower oil
6 soft-cooked or hard-cooked eggs
1 cup cherry tomatoes, halved
18 small button mushrooms
watercress sprigs

Place in a blender container the egg, lemon juice, vinegar, salt, mustard, tarragon, parsley, shallot, spinach and watercress. Blend until almost smooth. Gradually pour in oil in a fine steady stream, blending to make a thick mayonnaise. To serve, arrange whole soft-or hard-cooked eggs in each of 6 small ramekins and surround with tomatoes, mushrooms and watercress sprigs. Spoon about 3 or 4 tablespoons mayonnaise over each serving.
Makes 6 servings

PIROSHKI

Hot cheese pastry encases a beef filling for a savory appetizer snack.

1 small onion, minced
2 tablespoons butter
3/4 pound ground chuck, or
1-1/2 cups ground cooked veal or chicken
2 hard-cooked eggs, chopped
2 tablespoons minced parsley
1/2 teaspoon crumbled dried tarragon
1 clove garlic, minced
1/3 cup sour cream
Cream Cheese Pastry, following
1 egg white, lightly beaten

Sauté onion in butter until glazed. Add beef or other meats and cook through, if uncooked. Mix in eggs, parsley, tarragon, garlic and sour cream. Roll out pastry thinly and cut in 2-1/2-inch rounds with a fluted cutter. Put a teaspoonful of filling in the middle of each round, moisten edges and fold up to make a boat shape, with the seam on top. Place on a lightly greased baking sheet and brush with beaten egg white. Bake in a 400° oven for 15 to 20 minutes, or until golden.
Makes about 4 dozen

Cream Cheese Pastry Beat together 4 ounces cream cheese and 1/4 pound butter until creamy. Beat in 2 tablespoons heavy cream. Mix in 1-1/4 cups all-purpose flour and 1/2 teaspoon salt. Shape into a ball, wrap and chill 30 minutes.

Hors d'Oeufs

VIENNESE CHEESE DIAMONDS

These sophisticated cheese diamonds make a delightful accompaniment to a soup or salad luncheon.

3 eggs, separated
1/2 teaspoon salt
2 tablespoons butter, melted
3 tablespoons all-purpose flour
3/4 cup shredded Swiss cheese
4 ounces cream cheese, at room temperature
1/2 cup sour cream
3/4 cup cooked shrimp, crab meat or
    chopped ham
1/2 teaspoon grated lemon peel
1 tablespoon each chopped parsley and
    green onions
parsley sprigs

Beat together egg whites and salt until stiff, but not dry, and set aside. Beat egg yolks until thick and lemon colored and beat in butter and flour. Fold in egg whites and Swiss cheese. Butter a 9-inch square pan, line with waxed paper, and then butter waxed paper. Pour in batter. Bake in a 350° oven for 15 to 18 minutes, or until set. Turn out of pan and peel off paper. Let cool. Beat cream cheese until light and mix in sour cream, shrimp, lemon peel, parsley and onions. Spread over the cheese square and cut in diamonds. Garnish each diamond with a parsley sprig.
Makes about 2-1/2 dozen pieces

CHEESE PITAS
(Tiropitas)

Paper-thin fila dough makes a marvelous crispy wrapper for hot cheese appetizers. Make them in advance and freeze if you like, then reheat when you need them.

8 ounces each cream cheese and ricotta cheese
1/2 cup grated Parmesan cheese
3/4 cup shredded Gruyère or Samsoe cheese
1 egg
1 egg yolk
2 tablespoons chopped parsley
1 green onion, chopped
salt and pepper to taste
9 sheets fila dough
melted butter

Beat together the cheeses, egg, egg yolk, parsley, onion and salt and pepper. Lay out fila dough and cover with plastic wrap. Take out 1 sheet of fila and cut sheet into 4 strips. Brush strips with melted butter and fold each strip in half lengthwise. Brush again with butter. Place a rounded teaspoon of filling on one end of strip and fold over one corner to make a triangle. Continue folding pastry from side to side making a triangle. Place on a lightly buttered baking sheet. Repeat with remaining fila and filling. Brush tops with butter. Bake in a 375° oven for 15 minutes or until golden brown. Serve hot.
Makes 3 dozen

CHEESE AND CRAB QUICHES

Here is a buttery, press-in cheese pastry based on Gruyère. It is perfect for tiny appetizer tarts. Vary the filling, using different seafoods, ham or bacon.

1 cup all-purpose flour
1/4 teaspoon salt
2-1/4 cups finely shredded Gruyère or
   Samsoe cheese
6 tablespoons butter
2 egg yolks
3 eggs
1 cup half-and-half
6 ounces (1 cup) fresh cooked crab meat or
   shrimp, or
3/4 cup diced cooked ham or 6 strips bacon,
   cooked crisp and crumbled
dash each salt, pepper and ground nutmeg

For pastry, place in a mixing bowl the flour, salt and 1-1/4 cups of the cheese, and cut in butter until the consistency of fine crumbs. Make a well in the center and add egg yolks, mixing until it forms a ball. Pinch off small pieces and pat into the bottom and sides of small 1-1/2-inch tart pans.

    To make the filling, beat the eggs and blend in half-and-half. Mix in seafood, remaining cup of cheese, salt, pepper and nutmeg. Pour into tart shells, filling each 3/4 full. Bake in a 375° oven 20 to 25 minutes or until puffed and golden brown.
Makes about 2-1/2 dozen tarts

CRAB-FILLED MUSHROOMS

A hot seafood filling stuffs these butter-glazed mushroom caps.

1 pound mushrooms, about 1 inch in diameter
5 tablespoons butter
2 eggs
2 slices firm white bread (crusts removed),
   crumbled
3 tablespoons sour cream
6 ounces (1 cup) fresh cooked crab meat or
   shrimp, or
1 6-ounce can crab meat or shrimp, drained
1/2 teaspoon crumbled dried tarragon
1 green onion, chopped
1 tablespoon minced parsley
salt and pepper to taste
1/4 cup shredded Parmesan or Romano cheese

Remove stems from mushrooms and finely chop; set mushroom caps aside. Sauté chopped stems in 2 tablespoons of the butter just until glazed. Beat eggs until blended and mix in sautéed mushrooms, bread crumbs, sour cream, crab, tarragon, onion, parsley and salt and pepper to taste. Melt remaining butter and sauté mushroom caps until glazed. Place caps, cup side up, in a buttered baking dish. Pile crab filling in each one and sprinkle with cheese. Bake in a 375° oven for 10 minutes or until filling is set.
Makes about 3 dozen

Hors d'Oeufs

SAUSAGE IN BRIOCHE

A wonderful egg-rich brioche dough encases plump Italian sausages for a captivating appetizer or charming entrée.

10 mild Italian sausages (approximately 2 pounds)
1 package active dry yeast
1/2 cup lukewarm water (110° to 115°)
1 tablespoon sugar
1/4 teaspoon salt
2-1/2 cups all-purpose flour
3 eggs
1/4 pound butter, at room temperature
1 egg white, lightly beaten

Simmer sausage in water to cover for 20 minutes; drain and chill. Sprinkle yeast into warm water in a large mixing bowl and let stand until dissolved. Add sugar, salt and 1/2 cup of the flour and beat well. Add eggs, one at a time, and beat until smooth. Add butter and beat until blended. Gradually add remaining flour and beat hard 5 minutes. Cover with a towel and let rise in a warm place 1 hour. Punch down, cover with foil and chill 1 hour or longer. Divide dough into 10 pieces and roll out one piece into a rectangle about 1/4 inch thick. Place a sausage on the dough and roll up. Pinch ends to seal. Place seam side down on a greased baking sheet and repeat with remaining dough and sausages. Use a small aspic cutter to cut out crescents, stars or other designs from dough scraps and place on top of rolls. Cover with a towel and let rise in a warm place 20 minutes. Brush each roll with beaten egg white and bake in a 375° oven for 20 minutes, or until browned. Cut each sausage roll in 1/2-inch-thick slices and serve as appetizers, or leave whole as an entrée.
Makes about 5 dozen appetizers,
or 10 entrée servings

TOMATOES STUFFED WITH PEA MOUSSE

Here is a beautiful first course, vegetable dish or appetizer. The grass-green pea purée makes a striking center inside the tomatoes or neat little mushroom caps.

1-1/2 pounds peas, shelled, or
1 10-ounce package frozen petite peas, thawed
1/4 cup heavy cream
2 egg yolks
1 shallot or green onion, chopped
1 tablespoon butter
6 tablespoons shredded Romano or
    Parmesan cheese
4 large tomatoes

Cook peas in boiling salted water until tender; drain. Turn into a blender container and blend with cream, egg yolks, shallot, butter and 4 tablespoons of the cheese. Cut tomatoes in half and hollow out part of the insides, leaving a 3/4-inch-thick shell. Arrange tomato halves, hollow side up, in a buttered baking dish and spoon in pea purée. Sprinkle with remaining cheese. Bake in a 350° oven for 20 to 30 minutes or until set. Slip under the broiler and broil just until golden brown.
Makes about 8 first course or vegetable servings

Mushrooms Stuffed with Pea Mousse Remove stems from 24 mushroom caps, about 1-1/2 inches in diameter, and sauté caps in 1 tablespoon butter until glazed. Arrange in a baking dish and spoon in pea purée. Sprinkle with cheese and bake as directed above.

29

Hors d'Oeufs

EGG AND OLIVE CAVIAR SANDWICHES

Party-size rye forms the basis for these make-your-own, first-course sandwiches.

4 hard-cooked eggs
1 4-1/2-ounce can chopped ripe olives
1 2-ounce can red caviar
sour cream
finely chopped green onions or shallots
thinly sliced cocktail rye bread
sweet butter

Peel eggs and separate yolks from whites. Chop whites and press yolks through a fine sieve; place each in a bowl. Spoon olives, caviar, sour cream and onions into individual bowls. To serve, place bread in a basket and set out butter. Surround with bowls of ingredients for concocting open-face caviar sandwiches.
Makes 6 to 8 first-course servings

QUICK WINE CHEESE PUFF

Here is a fast, hot appetizer that calls for ingredients generally on hand. The golden brown puff cuts into neat wedges for serving.

3 eggs
2/3 cup all-purpose flour
1/3 cup dry white wine
2/3 cup milk
1/2 teaspoon salt
1 shallot or green onion, finely chopped
3/4 cup grated Swiss cheese
1 tablespoon butter, melted
2 tablespoons grated Parmesan cheese

Beat eggs until light and mix in flour, wine, milk, salt, shallot, Swiss cheese and butter. Pour into a buttered 9-inch pie pan and sprinkle with Parmesan. Bake in a 425° oven for 30 to 35 minutes or until puffed and golden brown. Cut in wedges.
Makes 16 to 18 appetizers

PÂTÉ DE CAMPAGNE

Spicy sausage stripes this cold pâté for an enticing picnic entrée. Or serve the pâté as a first course along with little French gherkins and crusty sourdough bread.

2 Italian garlic sausages
2 large onions, finely chopped
3 tablespoons butter
2 cloves garlic, minced
1/2 teaspoon each crumbled dried thyme and
   marjoram
1/4 teaspoon each ground allspice and nutmeg
1/8 teaspoon ground cloves
1-1/2 teaspoons salt
3/4 pound chicken livers
1 pound ground veal
1/2 pound ground pork
3 eggs, beaten
1/4 cup brandy or Cognac
3/4 cup heavy cream
2 bay leaves
8 to 10 peppercorns
finely chopped parsley

Cover sausages with water and simmer 20 minutes; drain. Sauté onions in butter until golden. Remove from heat and mix in garlic, thyme, marjoram, allspice, nutmeg, cloves and salt. Finely chop chicken livers and place in a bowl with veal, pork, eggs, brandy, cream and onion mixture. Mix until blended. Pat half of the mixture into a 9- by 5-inch terrine or loaf pan. Lay whole sausages end to end down the center and cover with remaining mixture. Garnish with bay leaves and peppercorns. Cover top of pan with foil. Place in a pan containing 1/2 inch hot water and bake in a 350° oven 2 hours. Remove foil and bake 15 minutes longer. Let cool slightly, then cover with foil, weight down and chill overnight before slicing. Sprinkle with parsley and serve from terrine. Pass French bread and a crock of sweet butter.
Makes 10 to 12 servings

Hors d'Oeufs

PETITE STEAK TARTARE

Cocktail rye bread forms the base for diminutive beef tartare sandwiches. On the tray, offer one or two egg yolks nestled in egg shells for those who wish to enrich their appetizer further.

1/2 pound ground sirloin or top round of beef
1 egg yolk
1/2 teaspoon each salt, Worcestershire sauce and
    Dijon-style mustard
1 tablespoon olive oil
1/2 teaspoon each chopped parsley and red onions
1 clove garlic, minced
butter
1 loaf thinly sliced cocktail rye bread
2 small red onions, sliced and separated into rings
parsley sprigs
1 or 2 egg yolks, nestled in egg shell halves

Mix together the ground beef, 1 egg yolk, salt, Worcestershire, mustard, oil, parsley, chopped onions and garlic. Lightly butter the cocktail bread and place an onion ring on each slice. Mound a spoonful of steak tartare in the center. Garnish with a sprig of parsley. Accompany with egg shells filled with yolks, letting guests spoon a tiny portion of the egg yolk on tartare before eating.
Makes about 2 to 3 dozen appetizers

SWISS CRUSTS
(Croûtes Suisse)

Wine-soaked, butter-browned bread rounds topped with a Gruyère sauce make a delightful hot first course for a cool meal. Assemble them in advance and pop them in to bake at the last minute.

6 slices Swiss Egg Bread (Coffee Can Variation,
    page 171), or other rich white bread
6 tablespoons butter
1/4 cup dry white wine
1/4 cup all-purpose flour
2 cups milk, heated
1/2 teaspoon salt
dash each pepper and ground nutmeg
3 egg yolks
1-1/2 cups shredded Gruyère or Samsoe cheese

Remove crusts from bread and trim slices to fit ramekins. Brown the bread in 2 tablespoons of the butter until golden but still soft inside. Arrange in buttered ramekins and saturate with wine. Melt remaining butter and stir in flour; cook 2 minutes. Gradually stir in milk, salt, pepper and nutmeg. Stirring, cook until thickened. Beat egg yolks and blend in part of the sauce; stir into remaining sauce. Add cheese and spoon sauce over wine-soaked bread. Bake in a 400° oven for 10 minutes or until golden brown.
Makes 6 servings

Soups

Soups

GREEK LEMON SOUP

The renowned Greek lemon soup depends on eggs for its creamy richness. The secret here is not to overheat the mixture or it will curdle. The first recipe is a quick first-course dish; the second can serve as a complete entrée.

GREEK LEMON SOUP—SIMPLIFIED

3 cups rich chicken broth
4 eggs
3 tablespoons freshly squeezed lemon juice

Heat chicken broth to boiling. Beat eggs in a large mixing bowl with a wire whisk and beat in the lemon juice. Gradually stir half of the broth into the eggs, whisking constantly. Return egg mixture to the saucepan, place over very low heat, and heat until soup is thickened, stirring frequently. Pour into small cups to serve.
Makes 6 first-course servings

CHICKEN SOUP WITH AVGOLEMONO SAUCE

1 3-pound fryer chicken
1 carrot, 1 onion and 1 celery stalk, cut up
salt and a few peppercorns
3 tablespoons long-grain rice
4 eggs, separated
1/3 cup freshly squeezed lemon juice

Wash fryer and place in a large soup kettle. Cover with about 1-1/2 quarts of water and add carrot, onion and celery stalk, salt to taste and a few peppercorns. Cover and simmer for 1 to 1-1/4 hours, or until chicken is tender. Remove chicken from broth and let cool slightly; remove meat from bones, discarding bones and skin, and tear meat into thin strips. Strain broth and skim extra fat. Return broth to kettle, add rice to broth and simmer until rice is tender. Beat egg whites until stiff. Beat yolks until light and fold into whites. Mix lemon juice into eggs. Pour part of the broth into the egg mixture, stirring to combine, and return to pan. Heat over low heat, beating with a wire whisk just until thickened. Return as much chicken as desired to the soup and heat through.
Makes 6 to 8 generous entrée servings

GREEK FISH SOUP

A lemon-egg sauce lends tang and body to this nourishing fish and vegetable soup.

1 onion, 1 carrot and 1 celery stalk, chopped
2 tablespoons olive oil
4 cups water
2 cups clam juice
1 cup dry white wine
salt and pepper to taste
1 2-1/2-pound piece halibut or other firm white fish
12 small new potatoes
3 leeks, trimmed to 6 inches in length, and
   cut in half lengthwise
4 eggs
1/4 cup freshly squeezed lemon juice

Using a large soup kettle, sauté onion, carrot and celery in oil until glazed. Add water, clam juice, wine and salt and pepper, and bring to a boil. Tie fish in cheesecloth and add along with potatoes to kettle; cover and simmer 10 minutes. Add leeks and simmer 10 minutes longer or until fish flakes with a fork. Remove fish and vegetables to a hot serving platter and keep warm. Beat together eggs and lemon juice and pour some of the hot broth into the egg mixture, stirring to combine thoroughly. Return to the pan and cook, stirring, over very low heat until thickened. Serve soup as a first course and follow with the fish and vegetables.
Makes 6 servings

SWISS CHEESE SKI SOUP

Here is a great after-ski soup. Accompany with little sausages grilled over the fire, fresh fruit and toasted marshmallows.

1 small onion, chopped
2 tablespoons butter
3 cups chicken broth
1-1/2 cups grated Swiss cheese
1 cup half-and-half
3 eggs
salt and pepper to taste
chopped parsley or green onions for garnish

Using a large soup kettle, sauté onion in butter until golden. Add broth and cheese, and heat until cheese melts. Turn into a blender and blend 30 seconds. Return to pan. Blend together half-and-half and eggs, mix in part of the cheese mixture, and return to pan. Cook and stir over very low heat until thickened. Season with salt and pepper. Serve in mugs and garnish with parsley or onions.
Makes 6 servings

Soups

STRACCIATELLA

Roman restaurants serve this simple, yet refined scrambled egg soup, strewn with Parmesan cheese and parsley.

4 cups rich beef or chicken stock
2 eggs
1/3 cup freshly shredded Parmesan or
   Romano cheese
2 tablespoons minced parsley
2 teaspoons chopped fresh basil, or
1/2 teaspoon crumbled dried basil
shredded Parmesan cheese for garnish

Heat broth to boiling. Beat eggs with cheese, parsley and basil. Pour mixture into the bubbling broth and immediately remove from heat; do not stir. Ladle into soup bowls and pass additional cheese. Makes 4 first-course servings

MARITATA SOUP

Italian maritata, or matrimonial soup, is an elegant first course to sip in the garden or living room as a prelude to dinner.

4 tablespoons sweet butter, at room temperature
1/2 cup each grated Monterey Jack cheese and
   Romano cheese
4 egg yolks
1 cup heavy cream
4 cups rich chicken stock
1 cup dry white wine
chopped parsley

Beat butter until creamy; then mix in cheeses, egg yolks and cream, beating well. Heat broth and wine until boiling. Ladle a spoonful of broth into the creamy cheese mixture and stir to combine thoroughly. Then stir cheese mixture into the hot broth. Place over low heat until just heated through. Sprinkle with parsley.

ZUPPA ALLA PAVESE

A poached egg floats on top of crunchy garlic bread in this Italian first-course soup.

3 tablespoons butter
1 clove garlic, mashed
4 slices Italian or French bread
1/3 cup grated Parmesan cheese
3-1/2 cups chicken stock
4 eggs, poached

Blend together butter and garlic and spread over the bread slices. Toast in a 350° oven for 15 minutes, or until golden and crusty. Sprinkle each piece of toast with some of the cheese and broil until cheese melts. Bring broth to a boil and ladle into bowls. Float a slice of toast in each bowl and slip a poached egg on top.
Makes 4 servings

JAPANESE EGG SOUP

The Japanese style of floating a few ingredients artistically in soup is eye-catching here.

6 cups clear chicken broth
1 tablespoon soy sauce
1 teaspoon freshly squeezed lemon juice
1/4 teaspoon shredded ginger root
6 snow peas
2 mushrooms, thinly sliced
1 green onion, thinly sliced
6 eggs

Heat together the chicken broth, soy sauce, lemon juice and ginger root and simmer 10 minutes. Add snow peas, mushrooms and onion. Carefully break eggs into the broth and poach just until set. Gently transfer eggs to soup bowls and ladle the broth and vegetables over them.
Makes 6 servings

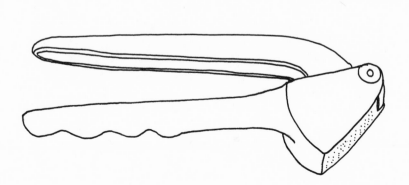

Soups

ALBONDIGAS SOUP

Flavor-packed little meatballs turn this Mexican vegetable soup into a full meal. Accompany with hot rolled tortillas and a fresh fruit plate of pineapple, papaya and melon.

8 cups beef or chicken stock
2 dried red chile peppers, seeded
1 onion, finely chopped
3/4 pound each ground beef and pork
1 teaspoon salt
2 eggs
1/4 cup all-purpose flour
4 carrots, peeled and grated
3 medium-sized zucchini, thinly sliced
2 large tomatoes, peeled and chopped
salt and freshly ground pepper to taste
chopped fresh coriander for garnish

Using a large soup pot, bring to a boil the stock, peppers and onion. Simmer 10 minutes. While broth is simmering, mix together the beef, pork, 1 teaspoon of salt, eggs and flour and shape into 1-inch balls. Add carrots, zucchini and tomatoes to the broth. Drop meatballs into the broth and simmer about 15 minutes or until vegetables are tender and meatballs are cooked through. Season with salt and pepper and sprinkle with coriander.
Makes 6 servings

ONION SOUP LYONNAISE STYLE

This gratinéed soup calls for a finishing flourish at the table. Crack an opening in the topping and blend in the medley of egg yolks and wine.

2 large onions, thinly sliced
2 tablespoons butter
4 cups rich beef or chicken stock
salt and freshly ground pepper to taste
4 slices sourdough French bread, spread with
   garlic butter and toasted
1 cup grated Gruyère or Swiss cheese
3 egg yolks
1/2 cup port wine

Using a large saucepan, sauté onions in butter until glazed and golden. Add stock and salt and pepper and cover and simmer 10 minutes. Break the toast into several pieces and place half of it in a buttered baking dish or casserole. Cover with half the cheese and pour in the soup. Cover with remaining toast and top with remaining cheese. Bake in a 400° oven for 25 to 30 minutes, or until golden brown. Beat egg yolks and blend in port. Bring soup and egg mixture to the table. Make a hole in the top of the soup and pour in the egg mixture, gently folding it into the soup.
Makes 4 to 6 servings

BEEF SOUP WITH EIERSTICH

Strips of egg custard, called Eierstich, garnish this full-meal beef and vegetable soup.

2 pounds beef shank
1 pound soup bones (with marrow, if possible)
salt and pepper to taste
2 bouillon cubes
1 leek, sliced
3 parsley sprigs
3 carrots, sliced
1 1-1/2-pound celery root, cut in 1/2-inch cubes
1/3 cup macaroni (optional)
1/4 teaspoon ground nutmeg
1 teaspoon soy sauce
Eierstich, following

Place beef shank and bones in a large soup pot and cover with water. Add salt and pepper and bouillon cubes. Cover and simmer 2 hours. Lift meat and soup bones from stock. Remove meat from bones and dice; set aside. Skim fat from stock, or, if possible, chill stock until fat solidifies and lift off. Bring stock to a boil and add leek, parsley, carrots, celery root, macaroni, nutmeg and soy sauce. Cover and simmer 15 to 20 minutes, or until vegetables are tender. Return meat to pot and heat through. Ladle into bowls and garnish with strips of Eierstich.
Makes 8 servings

EIERSTICH

2 eggs
3 tablespoons milk
1/2 teaspoon salt
dash ground nutmeg

Beat eggs until blended and mix in milk, salt and nutmeg. Lightly butter the top of a double boiler and pour in custard. Cover and cook over simmering water just until set, about 20 to 25 minutes. Cut into strips or dice in the pan, lift out with a spatula and use as a soup garnish.

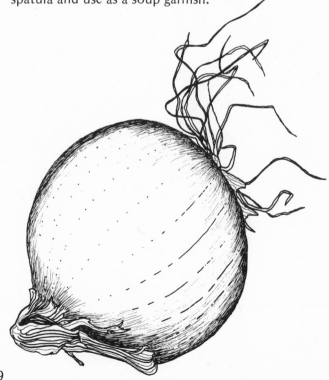

Soups

WATERCRESS SOUP

This slightly spicy, pale-green soup is a superb starter for poached salmon or roast lamb.

1 medium-sized onion, chopped
3 tablespoons butter
2 medium-sized potatoes, peeled and cut in cubes
4 cups chicken stock
1 bunch watercress (approximately 4 ounces)
2 egg yolks
1 cup half-and-half
salt and pepper to taste
dash ground nutmeg
sour cream for garnish

Using a large saucepot, sauté onion in butter until glazed. Add potatoes and stock, cover and simmer 15 minutes. Add sprigs of watercress and simmer 2 minutes longer. Let cool slightly, then purée in a blender. Return to the pan. Blend together egg yolks and half-and-half and stir in. Season with salt, pepper and nutmeg. Stirring, cook until thickened over low heat. Ladle into mugs and garnish with sour cream.
Makes 8 servings

CREAM OF SPINACH SOUP

Cook this bright green soup briefly so it retains its lovely verdant color.

4 green onions, finely chopped (use only half
   the green tops)
2 tablespoons butter
2 tablespoons flour
3 cups rich chicken broth
1 bunch spinach, finely chopped (about 2 cups)
1/8 teaspoon ground nutmeg
salt and pepper to taste
3 egg yolks
1/3 cup heavy cream
sour cream or plain yogurt for topping

Using a large saucepan, sauté onions in butter until glazed. Stir in flour and cook 2 minutes. Gradually pour in stock and cook until thickened and smooth, stirring with a whisk. Add spinach, nutmeg and salt and pepper and cook 2 minutes. Beat egg yolks, blend in cream and ladle in a little of the hot soup, mixing well. Return to the saucepan and cook over very low heat, just until thickened. Serve hot in bowls, each topped with a dollop of sour cream or yogurt.
Makes 6 servings

MUSHROOM BISQUE

This creamy, sherry-scented soup makes a fine prelude to dinner. Serve it in small mugs, tea cups or stoneware bowls, in the living room if you wish.

1 small onion, finely chopped
3 tablespoons butter
1/2 pound mushrooms, coarsely chopped
    (approximately 2 cups)
3 tablespoons flour
2 cups rich chicken stock
1/4 cup dry white wine
1/2 teaspoon crumbled dried tarragon
1 clove garlic, minced
salt and pepper to taste
2 cups rich milk or half-and-half
3 egg yolks
1/4 cup pale dry sherry
sour cream
parsley sprigs

Using a large saucepan, sauté onion in butter until golden. Add mushrooms and sauté until glazed. Stir in flour and cook 2 minutes. Add stock, wine, tarragon, garlic, salt and pepper and bring to a boil; simmer 10 minutes. Purée in a blender until mushrooms are very finely chopped. Return to saucepan. Purée milk with egg yolks and blend in part of the mushroom mixture, stirring to combine thoroughly. Return to pan, add sherry and cook and stir over very low heat until thickened. Serve in bowls and garnish with sour cream and parsley.
Makes 8 servings

ASPARAGUS SOUP

Here is a spring soup to time with asparagus season. Let it begin a party dinner featuring roast lamb.

1 pound asparagus
3 cups rich chicken stock
2 tablespoons each butter and flour
3 egg yolks
1/3 cup heavy cream
salt and freshly ground pepper to taste
1/2 teaspoon crumbled dried tarragon

Peel the asparagus stalks. Cut off only the very tips and cook them in boiling salted water for 3 minutes; drain and reserve. Cut the peeled stalks into 1-inch lengths and cook in chicken stock for 20 minutes, or until very tender. Purée broth and stalks in a blender; set aside. Melt butter, blend in flour and cook 2 minutes. Add the asparagus purée and cook for about 10 minutes, or until mixture is smooth and thick. Beat egg yolks and blend in cream. Ladle a little of the hot soup into the yolks, stirring well, and return to the pan. Cook and stir over low heat just until thickened. Season with salt, pepper and tarragon and add the asparagus tips. Ladle into bowls and serve.
Makes 6 servings

Soups

ICED SUMMER SOUP

This cool soup has a low-calorie, buttermilk base.

1 quart buttermilk
1/2 teaspoon each salt and Worcestershire sauce
1 tablespoon freshly squeezed lemon juice
dash Tabasco sauce
1 large cucumber, peeled and chopped
2 green onions, chopped
2 hard-cooked eggs, finely chopped
3 ounces (1/2 cup) small fresh cooked shrimp
minced parsley

In a large container combine the buttermilk with the salt, Worcestershire, lemon juice and Tabasco. Add the cucumber, onions, eggs and shrimp and mix lightly. Serve chilled, garnished with parsley.
Makes 6 servings

JELLIED BORSCH

For novelty, offer a selection of condiments with this tangy summer soup. Let it be the star at supper with cold meats, dark rye and fresh peaches or nectarines.

1 pound beets
1 envelope unflavored gelatin
1 cup pickle juice (preferably from bread-and-
   butter pickles)
1-1/4 cups rich beef stock
3 tablespoons chopped sweet red or white onion
salt and pepper to taste
1/2 teaspoon Worcestershire sauce
1/8 teaspoon each ground cloves and allspice
sour cream
3 hard-cooked eggs, sieved
3 green onions, chopped
red or black caviar

Cut tops from beets and cook beets in boiling water until tender; reserve juice and peel and shred beets. Dissolve gelatin in pickle juice; heat to boiling and stir in beef stock, beet juice, onion, salt, pepper, Worcestershire, cloves and allspice. Remove from heat and stir in beets. Chill until cold and syrupy. Ladle into soup bowls and pass bowls of sour cream, eggs, onions and caviar for garnish.
Makes 6 servings

Salads & Vegetables

Salads & Vegetables

ITALIAN TELEME, TOMATO AND EGG SALAD

Sliced hard-cooked eggs are a welcome bonus to the traditional Italian tricolor salad. It is a combination of cheese, tomatoes and pungently fresh sweet basil. Creamy Teleme cheese is a proper substitute for the fresh Mozzarella the Italians use. Offer this salad after a pasta supper—as a combination salad-cheese course.

3 large tomatoes, sliced
1/4 pound Teleme or Mozzarella cheese, sliced
3 hard-cooked eggs, sliced
leaves from 1 small bunch fresh basil
olive oil
salt and freshly ground pepper

Place overlapping circles of sliced tomatoes around a large platter. Arrange a slice of cheese on top of each circle and place sliced eggs on the cheese slices. Place basil leaves in the center of the platter, overlapping the egg slices. Drizzle with oil and season with salt and pepper. Serve each person a composite of the 4 major ingredients.
Makes 6 servings

SWISS PEPPER AND EGG SALAD

This hearty picnic salad needs only French bread, dill pickles and salami for accompaniments. Finish off with fruit and cookies.

1/2 pound Gruyère, Samsoe or Jarlsberg cheese, cut in julienne
8 hard-cooked eggs, chopped
1 red bell pepper, diced
2 green onions, chopped
1/4 cup chopped parsley
3/4 cup sour cream
2 teaspoons Dijon-style mustard
dash each salt and freshly ground pepper
2 tablespoons capers
romaine

Place cheese and chopped eggs in a bowl with pepper, onions and parsley. Mix together the sour cream, mustard, salt, pepper and capers, pour over cheese mixture and mix lightly. Chill. To serve, spoon into a bowl lined with romaine leaves, or spoon some of the egg mixture on the inner leaves of a head of romaine, fold up and eat out of hand.
Makes 4 servings

EGGS IN ASPIC

Poached eggs sit in shimmering aspic for a charming luncheon salad or first course.

1 envelope unflavored gelatin
1/4 cup cold water
1-1/2 cups rich chicken stock
1/4 cup dry white wine
4 to 6 poached eggs
capers and sliced pimiento-stuffed green olives
    for garnish (optional)
watercress
sour cream
chopped chives
cherry tomatoes

Soften gelatin in cold water. Combine stock and wine and heat to boiling; stir in gelatin. Remove from heat and stir until dissolved. Chill. Coat the interior of small individual molds with a layer of aspic and chill until congealed. Place a cooled poached egg in the center of each and fill with more aspic. Garnish top with capers and sliced pimiento-stuffed olives, if desired. Chill until set. Unmold and place on a bed of watercress and garnish each with a dollop of sour cream, a sprinkling of chives and a few cherry tomatoes.
Makes 4 to 6 servings

WESTERN COBB SALAD

This Western salad is often layered in a pyramid, but this presentation displays each ingredient like spokes of a wheel.

butter lettuce
4 hard-cooked eggs
8 strips of bacon, cooked crisp and crumbled
1 cup diced cooked chicken breast meat
2 medium-sized tomatoes, peeled and diced
1 large avocado, peeled and diced
1/2 cup crumbled blue or Roquefort cheese
 watercress sprigs (optional)
Vinaigrette Dressing, following

Arrange a bed of greens on 4 dinner plates. Peel eggs, dice whites and shred yolks, keeping them separate. On each plate of greens arrange 1 spoke each of the egg whites, egg yolks, bacon, chicken breast, tomatoes and avocado. Scatter cheese over the center and garnish with watercress. Pass dressing in a pitcher to pour over.
Makes 4 servings

Vinaigrette Dressing Shake together 2/3 cup safflower oil, 1/4 cup white wine vinegar, 1 tablespoon freshly squeezed lemon juice, and 1 teaspoon each salt and Dijon-style mustard.

Salads & Vegetables

SAUSAGE AND EGG BISTRO SALAD

Left Bank Parisian bistros offer a tantalizing combination of hot French sausages and slightly coddled eggs nestled in crisp greens as a first course.

1 cup French bread cubes
2 tablespoons butter
1 clove garlic, minced
1 head escarole, curly endive or romaine
1/4 cup olive oil or safflower oil
2 tablespoons white wine vinegar
1/2 teaspoon each salt and Dijon-style mustard
1 shallot or green onion, chopped
2 thick slices bacon, diced
2 mild Italian garlic sausages
2 eggs
1 tomato, cut in wedges

Sauté bread cubes in butter with garlic until golden brown. Let cool. Tear greens into bite-sized pieces and place in a salad bowl; chill. Mix together the oil, vinegar, salt, mustard and shallot and chill. Cook bacon until crisp, reserving drippings. Place sausages in a saucepan, cover with water, bring to a boil and let simmer 20 minutes. Drain, skin and slice on the diagonal; keep warm. Place eggs in a pan of cold water, bring just to boiling and barely simmer for 4 minutes; rinse under cold running water, shell and cut in quarters. (The centers should still be soft.) When ready to serve, pour hot bacon drippings and dressing over the greens. Add hot sausages and bacon and mix lightly. Garnish with eggs and tomato wedges and scatter over croûtons.
Makes 6 servings

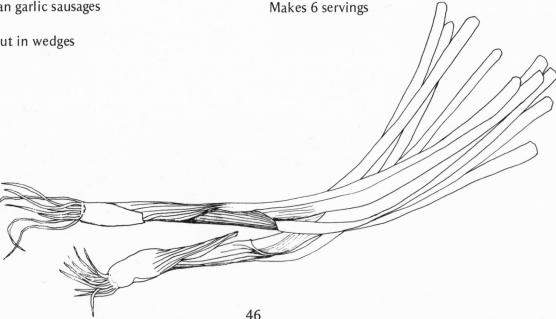

46

CAESAR SALAD GARNI

This famous Western salad can be embellished with protein—crab, shrimp, ham, salami, roast beef or chicken—to turn it into a summer entrée salad.

1 cup French bread cubes
2 tablespoons butter
1 clove garlic, bruised
1 large head romaine
3 tablespoons olive oil
1 egg
1-1/2 tablespoons freshly squeezed lemon juice
1/2 teaspoon Dijon-style mustard
1/4 teaspoon salt
freshly ground pepper to taste
4 anchovy fillets, chopped
1/2 cup freshly grated Parmesan cheese
1/2 pound small fresh cooked shrimp or other
    seafood or meat

Sauté bread cubes in butter with garlic until golden brown. Let cool. Tear romaine into a salad bowl. Combine in a blender the oil, egg, lemon juice, mustard, salt and pepper and blend until smooth. Pour over greens and mix lightly. Add anchovies, cheese, shrimp and reserved croûtons and mix lightly again.
Makes 4 servings

DUTCH SALAD

A spicy sour cream dressing makes a pleasant addition to greens embellished with hard-cooked eggs and Swiss cheese.

Sour Cream Dressing, following
1 head butter lettuce
1/3 pound Samsoe, Jarlsberg or Gruyère cheese,
    cut in julienne
3 hard-cooked eggs, sliced
watercress sprigs

First prepare dressing and set aside. Wash greens and tear into bite-sized pieces. Pour half the dressing over the greens and mix lightly. Spoon greens into a salad bowl and scatter over cheese and eggs. Ring with watercress sprigs. Spoon remaining dressing on top, to mix in as served.
Makes 6 servings

Sour Cream Dressing Combine 1/2 cup sour cream or plain yogurt, 1 tablespoon each Dijon-style mustard and chopped shallots, 2 tablespoons freshly squeezed lemon juice and 1/2 teaspoon ground cumin. Season with salt and pepper to taste.

Salads & Vegetables

PICNIC POTATO SALAD

A creamy dressing binds this old-fashioned style potato salad that is a favorite side dish to baked ham or cold meats.

5 large boiling potatoes, cooked, peeled and diced
5 hard-cooked eggs, sliced
2/3 cup finely chopped celery
1/4 cup chopped parsley
1 medium-sized dill pickle, diced
Mustard Dressing, following

Place in a salad bowl the potatoes, 3 sliced eggs, celery, parsley and pickle. Prepare Mustard Dressing as directed and spoon dressing over; mix lightly. Chill. Garnish with remaining eggs and serve.
Makes 6 to 8 servings

MUSTARD DRESSING

2 tablespoons each all-purpose flour and sugar
1 teaspoon each salt and dry mustard
1/2 teaspoon Dijon-style mustard
1/4 teaspoon paprika
3/4 cup water
1/4 cup cider vinegar
1 egg, lightly beaten
2 tablespoons butter, at room temperature

Mix together in the top of a double boiler the flour, sugar, salt, dry mustard, Dijon-style mustard and paprika. Stir in the water, vinegar and egg. Cook over simmering water, stirring, until sauce is thickened. Remove from heat and stir in butter. Let cool and chill. This is also good served over cooked and sliced Jerusalem artichokes.

SALAD CÔTE D'AZUR

This Provençal salad is perfect for a picnic luncheon with crusty French bread and a chilled bottle of white wine.

3/4 pound Italian-style green beans, trimmed
   and cut in 1-inch lengths, or
1 9-ounce package frozen Italian-style green beans
Shallot Dressing, following
1 medium-sized head butter lettuce or red
   leaf lettuce
1 6- or 7-ounce can white albacore tuna
2 hard-cooked eggs, sliced
3 tomatoes, cut in wedges
1 red or green bell pepper, sliced
1 small sweet red onion, sliced
8 anchovy fillets
12 Mediterranean olives (optional)

Cook beans in boiling salted water until crisp-tender; drain, let cool and pour over 1/4 cup of the Shallot Dressing. Chill.

Line salad bowl with outer leaves of lettuce and tear inner leaves into bite-sized pieces. Place marinated beans in the center. Top with tuna and surround with egg slices, tomatoes, pepper and onion. Garnish with anchovies and olives. If desired, cover and chill. When ready to serve, pour over desired amount of dressing and mix lightly.
Makes 4 servings

Shallot Dressing Mix together 1/4 cup red wine vinegar, 2/3 cup olive oil, 1/2 teaspoon salt, freshly ground pepper to taste, 1 shallot, chopped, and 1/2 teaspoon dried sweet basil or tarragon. Makes about 1 cup.

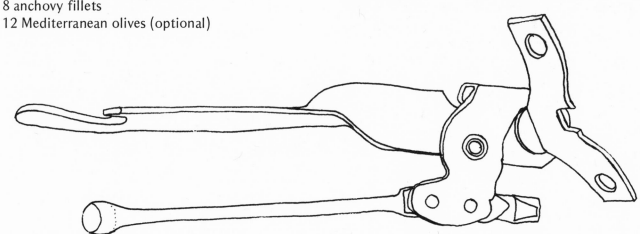

Salads & Vegetables

JERUSALEM ARTICHOKE AND EGG SALAD

Here is a novel picnic salad that travels well.

1/2 pound Jerusalem artichokes
1/2 pound mushrooms, thinly sliced (approximately 2 cups)
3 tablespoons chopped parsley
Shallot Dressing, page 49
2 or 3 hard-cooked eggs, quartered
2 tomatoes, cut in wedges
1 bunch watercress, approximately
    4 ounces (optional)

Scrub artichokes and cook whole in boiling salted water until tender, about 10 to 15 minutes; drain. When cool enough to handle, peel and slice 1/4 inch thick into a bowl. Add mushrooms and parsley and pour over enough Shallot Dressing to coat lightly. Cover and chill. When ready to serve, garnish with eggs and tomato wedges and tuck in watercress sprigs.
Makes 6 servings

MEXICAN CHICKEN OR SEAFOOD SALAD

Guacamole and sour cream make lively toppings on this chicken salad plate.

1 small head romaine
3 tablespoons olive oil
1-1/2 tablespoons white wine vinegar
1/2 teaspoon Dijon-style mustard
1/4 teaspoon salt
4 cold cooked split chicken breasts, boned
    and sliced, or
1 pound cooked crab meat or small shrimp
4 hard-cooked eggs, sliced
1 cup cherry tomatoes
8 radishes, trimmed, or pitted ripe olives
Guacamole, following
sour cream

Tear romaine into bite-sized pieces. Combine oil, vinegar, mustard and salt and toss with romaine. Spoon greens onto 4 salad plates. Arrange sliced chicken or seafood on the greens and garnish with eggs, tomatoes, and radishes or olives. Spoon a mound of Guacamole over each and top with a spoonful of sour cream.
Makes 4 servings

Guacamole Halve and seed 1 large avocado and scoop out pulp into a bowl. Mash pulp with 2 tablespoons each freshly squeezed lemon juice and chopped fresh coriander, 1 chopped green onion, 1 clove garlic, minced, and 1/4 teaspoon salt.

WILD RICE, EGG AND SHRIMP SALAD

Here is an extravagant salad. As options to shrimp, consider cooked chicken breast meat, ham, crab or lobster tails.

1/2 pound mushrooms, sliced (approximately
    2 cups)
2 tablespoons olive oil
1-1/2 tablespoons freshly squeezed lemon juice
3 cups cold cooked wild rice (or white and wild
    rice combination)
3 hard-cooked eggs, chopped
2 green onions, chopped
Garlic Mayonnaise, following
romaine
1 pound cooked medium-sized shrimp,
    shelled and deveined
1 cup cherry tomatoes

Sauté mushrooms in oil with lemon juice; let cool. Mix together lightly the mushrooms, rice, eggs, onions and Garlic Mayonnaise. Pile onto a salad bowl lined with romaine and garnish with shrimp and tomatoes.
Makes 6 servings

Garlic Mayonnaise Mix together 2 cloves garlic, crushed, 1/2 teaspoon Dijon-style mustard, 1/8 teaspoon pepper, 1/2 cup mayonnaise and 1/4 cup sour cream.

SHRIMP AND CELERY ROOT SALAD

Particularly dramatic for a holiday buffet table, this seafood salad may be assembled in advance.

1 2-pound celery root
1 6-ounce jar marinated artichoke hearts,
    drained (reserve marinade) and cut up
1/2 pound small cooked shrimp or crab meat
4 hard-cooked eggs, chopped
1/4 cup each mayonnaise and sour cream
1 tablespoon freshly squeezed lemon juice
2 teaspoons capers
1/2 teaspoon each grated lemon peel and
    crumbled dried tarragon
salt and pepper to taste
curly endive or romaine
1-1/2 cups cherry tomatoes, halved

Peel and slice celery root 1/2 inch thick and cook in boiling salted water for 20 minutes or until tender. Drain, cool and dice in 1/2-inch cubes; turn into bowl. Add the artichoke hearts and their marinade and mix lightly. Add shrimp and chopped eggs. Mix together the mayonnaise, sour cream, lemon juice, capers, lemon peel, tarragon, salt and pepper and pour over artichoke mixture, mixing lightly. Pile into a bowl lined with endive and scatter cherry tomatoes over all.
Makes 8 servings

Salads & Vegetables

SPINACH AND EGG SALAD

This colorful spinach salad is a bright addition to a buffet table.

1/4 cup each safflower oil and olive oil
1/4 cup red wine vinegar
1 clove garlic, minced
1/2 teaspoon salt
1 teaspoon Dijon-style mustard
freshly ground pepper
1 cup cherry tomatoes, halved
2 green onions, finely chopped
1 large bunch spinach (approximately 1 pound)
2 hard-cooked eggs, chopped or sieved

Combine in a bowl the oils, vinegar, garlic, salt, mustard and pepper, stirring to blend. Add cherry tomatoes and onions and let chill about 1 hour. Wash and trim spinach, tear leaves into pieces and chill. When ready to serve, mix spinach with tomatoes, onions and dressing in a salad bowl and sprinkle over the eggs.
Makes 6 servings

SPINACH RICOTTA BALLS

Cheese-filled spinach balls make a novel hot accompaniment to steak, roast beef or ham.

3 large bunches spinach (approximately 3 pounds),
    chopped and cooked until wilted, or
3 12-ounce packages frozen chopped spinach,
    thawed
2 tablespoons minced parsley
2 cloves garlic, minced
2 eggs
2 cups (1 pint) ricotta cheese
1 cup freshly shredded Parmesan cheese
1/2 cup dry French bread crumbs
flour
freshly grated Parmesan or Romano cheese

Squeeze out the moisture from the spinach thoroughly and mix in parsley and garlic. Beat eggs and mix in the ricotta, shredded Parmesan, bread crumbs and the spinach mixture. Shape into walnut-sized balls and roll in flour. Bring 2 quarts water to a boil, add a few balls at a time and simmer just until balls float to the top, about 10 minutes. Lift out to an ovenproof serving dish and keep warm while cooking remaining balls. Sprinkle balls with grated cheese just before serving. If desired, cook in advance and reheat in a 350° oven for 20 minutes or until heated through.
Makes 6 to 8 servings

SPINACH ROULADE

This beautiful spinach roll, spiraled with coral salmon, makes a choice vegetable side dish or luncheon entrée.

2 bunches spinach (approximately 2 pounds),
   chopped
3 green onions, finely chopped
2 tablespoons chopped parsley
2 tablespoons butter
5 eggs, separated
1/2 teaspoon salt
1 cup (1/2 pint) sour cream
1 cup shredded Romano or Parmesan cheese
2 tablespoons chopped shallots
2/3 cup diced smoked salmon or small fresh
   cooked shrimp (optional)

Using a large frying pan, cook spinach, onions and parsley in butter over medium-high heat until vegetables are barely wilted; drain off any extra juices. Beat egg whites until foamy, add salt and beat until soft peaks form. Beat egg yolks until thick and pale and beat in 1/3 cup of the sour cream and 1/2 cup of the cheese. Mix the spinach mixture into the yolk mixture and fold in the egg whites. Butter a 10- by 15-inch jelly-roll pan, line with waxed paper and butter paper heavily. Pour in the spinach mixture and sprinkle with remaining cheese. Bake in a 350° oven for 30 minutes or until set. Immediately turn out upside down on a kitchen towel, remove pan and peel off the waxed paper. Mix together the remaining sour cream, shallots and salmon (if desired) and spread over the spinach. Roll up, like a jelly-roll, from the lengthwise side. Place on a platter. Cut in 1-1/4-inch-thick slices and serve hot or at room temperature.
Makes 6 to 8 servings

Salads & Vegetables

DUTCH ASPARAGUS

Ribbons of sieved egg yolks, whites and minced watercress decorate an asparagus platter.

2 pounds asparagus
freshly grated nutmeg
4 tablespoons butter
2 hard-cooked eggs
1/2 cup minced watercress or parsley

Trim tough ends from asparagus and cook spears in boiling salted water for 5 to 7 minutes or until tender; drain. Arrange spears on a warm serving platter and grate a little nutmeg over them. Heat butter until bubbly and browned slightly and pour over asparagus. Separate yolks from whites and sieve each separately. Sprinkle ribbons of egg yolk, watercress and egg white over the asparagus. Serve at once.
Makes 6 servings

ZUCCHINI AUGUSTINO

Cheese and crumb-coated zucchini go well with broiled lamb chops or steak.

1-1/2 pounds medium-sized zucchini
2 eggs
1/2 teaspoon crumbled dried basil
salt and pepper to taste
1/2 cup fine dry bread crumbs
3 tablespoons grated Parmesan cheese
olive oil

Cut zucchini into 3/8-inch-thick slices. Beat eggs with basil, salt and pepper. Combine bread crumbs and cheese. Dip zucchini into eggs and then into cheese-crumb mixture. In a large frying pan, fry zucchini slices in 1/4 inch hot olive oil until richly browned. Remove to a baking sheet lined with paper toweling and keep warm until all are cooked.
Makes 4 to 6 servings

Cauliflower Variation Cook 1 whole medium-sized cauliflower in boiling salted water until crisp-tender; drain and separate into flowerets. Let cool. Then prepare in egg batter and fry as above.

MIXED VEGETABLE FRITTERS

The Italian way of frying batter-dipped vegetables in oil called fritto misto makes a choice accompaniment to broiled fish or roast chicken, beef or lamb.

2 medium-sized zucchini
2 medium-sized crookneck squash
1 small eggplant (approximately 1 pound)
12 small button mushrooms
salt to taste
flour
2 eggs, beaten
olive oil
parsley sprigs
1 lemon, thinly sliced

First prepare each of the vegetables for cooking. Cut zucchini diagonally into 3/8-inch-thick slices. Cut crookneck into lengthwise slices, about 1/4 inch thick. Slice eggplant crosswise 1/4 inch thick and cut each slice in half. Trim ends from mushroom caps. Season vegetables with salt, shake them in flour, then dip in beaten egg. Fry vegetables over medium-high heat in a large frying pan containing about 1/2 inch olive oil until each piece is richly browned. Remove to a baking sheet lined with paper toweling and keep warm in a low oven until all vegetables are cooked. Garnish each serving with parsley sprigs and lemon slices.
Makes 4 servings

EGGPLANT WITH PINE NUTS

A browned béchamel topping glazes eggplant slices for a gala accompaniment to roast lamb or chicken.

1 large eggplant
3 tablespoons olive oil
2 tablespoons each butter and flour
1 cup milk, heated
2 egg yolks
1/4 cup sour cream
2 ounces feta cheese, crumbled
1/4 cup grated Romano or Parmesan cheese
1/3 cup pine nuts

Cut eggplant crosswise into 1-inch-thick slices discarding ends. Brush both sides of each slice with oil and place in a shallow baking pan. Bake in a 450° oven for 20 minutes, turning once, or until tender.

Melt butter in a small saucepan and stir in flour; cook and stir 2 minutes. Gradually pour in milk and stirring, cook until thickened. Beat egg yolks and sour cream together, stir in some of the hot sauce and return to pan. Add cheeses and cook and stir just until thickened. Spread cheese sauce over eggplant slices and sprinkle with nuts. Place in a 450° oven until topping browns lightly.
Makes 6 servings

Whole Egg Entrees

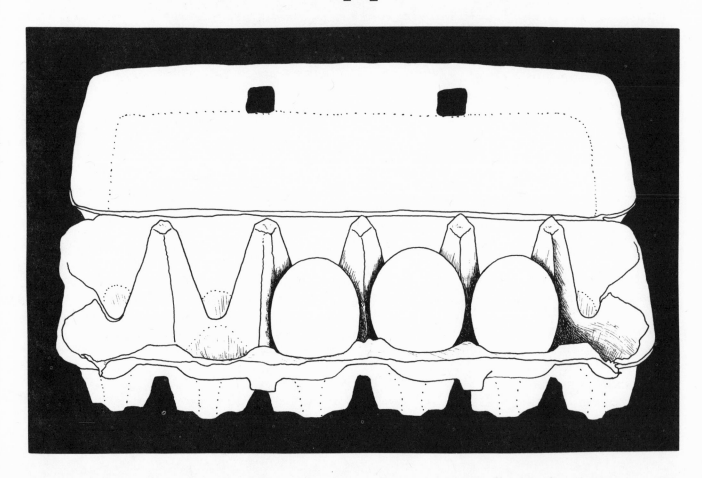

SOFT-COOKED AND HARD-COOKED EGGS

There are several methods for cooking eggs in the shell, but the most important factors are not to cook them in boiling water or for too long a time. Extra-high heat and overcooking cause rubbery whites, green-ringed yolks and cracked and leaking shells. It is best to start with room-temperature eggs as they are less likely to crack.

To soft-cook or hard-cook eggs you begin the same way. Place eggs in a saucepan and add enough cold tap water to cover the eggs by about 1 inch. Place pan, uncovered, over high heat and bring to a boil; then reduce the heat to simmer so that only an occasional bubble breaks on the bottom. For soft-cooked eggs with a firm white and a slightly set yolk that is still liquid in the center, figure 3 minutes from the time the water boils. If you prefer a yolk that is set through, allow 4 minutes. Remove from hot water immediately. For hard-cooked eggs, allow to simmer exactly 12 minutes, then drain off water and fill pan with cold water to stop their cooking.

A less desirable method for hard-cooking and soft-cooking eggs is to bring enough water to a boil so that the eggs will be covered by a generous inch, slip the eggs into the boiling water with a spoon, reduce heat to simmer and cook for 3 to 4 minutes for soft-cooked eggs and 12 to 15 minutes for hard-cooked eggs. Remove soft-cooked eggs at once from hot water. For hard-cooked eggs, remove from heat, drain off water and immediately cover with cold water to prevent further cooking and facilitate peeling.

Another method of hard-cooking eggs is to place the eggs in a saucepan, cover completely with cold water and bring water to a boil. At this point immediately cover pan and remove from heat. Let stand 20 minutes, then immerse in cold water. If you are cooking more than 6 eggs at once, let them stand 25 minutes before cooling.

Coddled eggs are a variation of soft-cooked eggs. Lower eggs into a pan of boiling water, remove from heat, cover pan and time. Allow 4 to 6 minutes depending on desired firmness.

Shelling a hard-cooked egg may be difficult only because it is too fresh. Tap it at the larger, blunt end where the air sac is located and start peeling at that end. It helps to shell eggs under cold running water. Eggs used to be coated heavily with oil to maintain freshness longer, and were therefore very difficult to shell. Now the egg industry oils eggs lightly enough to allow the acid-alkaline change to occur. Even so, occasionally an egg is inadvertently oiled heavily and the shell is difficult to remove.

Whole Egg Entrees

FRIED EGGS

A good fried egg should be tender and unbrowned on the bottom whether it is cooked sunny-side up or turned. Heat the frying pan over moderately high heat, add butter or margarine and break the egg directly into the pan, holding the shell almost against the surface of the pan and letting the egg slide out. If you want the white over the yolks to be cooked through, either baste it with hot pan drippings or turn the egg over; or add a few drops of water for each egg and cover the pan, letting the eggs lightly steam. To flip the egg, shake the pan gently to loosen the egg from the surface, using a spatula if necessary. Slide spatula under the center of the egg, lift and turn over. Cook to desired doneness: over easy, over medium or over hard. Some people prefer a quickly cooked egg, one that is cooked over high heat and is browned and crispy on the edges.

SHIRRED EGGS

A shirred egg differs from a baked egg in that it is first cooked on top of the stove and then placed in the oven or under the broiler briefly. For each serving, lightly butter a shallow flameproof dish and heat until butter melts. Break in 1 or 2 eggs and cook gently on top of the stove until bottom is set. Then place a few inches beneath a hot broiler or in a 450° oven for 45 to 50 seconds until the yolks are filmed over. The white should be softly set and the yolk still liquid. Remove from oven or broiler and season with salt and pepper to taste.

BAKED EGGS

To bake eggs, allow 1 or 2 eggs per serving and bake them in small individual porcelain, tempered glass or stoneware ramekins. Lightly butter the ramekin and pour 1 tablespoon of heavy cream in the bottom. Break in 1 or 2 eggs and spoon 1 tablespoon of heavy cream over top. Place in a pan of hot water and bake in a 375° oven for 7 to 10 minutes, or until eggs are set to your liking. Remove from the oven and the water bath and season with salt and pepper to taste.

Variations
• Add 1/2 to 1 teaspoon minced mixed fresh parsley, chives or tarragon to the cream.
• Add 3 tablespoons shredded Gruyère or Cheddar cheese to the cream.
• Place in the bottom of the buttered ramekin a little minced cooked mushrooms, asparagus spears, spinach or artichoke hearts, first mixed with a little cream or béchamel sauce.
• Mix fresh lobster, shrimp or crab meat with a little cream or béchamel sauce and place in bottom of ramekins before breaking in the eggs.

BAKED EGGS WITH MUSHROOMS

Eggs baked with ham or prosciutto make a festive dish for brunch.

thinly sliced cooked ham or prosciutto
    (approximately 3 ounces)
4 eggs
salt and pepper
1/3 pound mushrooms, sliced
1 shallot, chopped
2 tablespoons butter
1 tablespoon dry sherry
1/4 teaspoon crumbled dried tarragon
1/4 cup heavy cream
watercress sprigs

Line 4 small round baking dishes or custard cups (about 3/4 cup capacity) with ham. Break an egg into each one and sprinkle with salt and pepper. Place dishes in a pan containing 1/2 inch hot water and bake in a 350° oven for 20 to 25 minutes or until set. While eggs are baking, sauté mushrooms and chopped shallot in butter just until glazed. Add sherry, tarragon and cream and cook down until reduced to a glaze. Spoon glazed mushrooms around baked eggs and garnish with watercress.
Makes 4 servings

ASPARAGUS AND EGGS MILANESE

A springtime specialty in Milan is this lovely pairing of eggs and asparagus—simplicity at its best.

1-1/2 pounds large asparagus
4 tablespoons butter
8 eggs
salt and pepper
1/4 cup diced prosciutto or cooked ham
1/2 cup shredded Parmesan cheese

Trim tough ends from asparagus and cook spears in boiling salted water until tender, about 5 to 7 minutes; drain. Divide butter among 4 individual oval baking dishes or ramekins and heat in a 350° oven. Break 2 eggs into center of each dish, sprinkle with salt and pepper and return to the oven until whites are just set, about 8 minutes. Remove from oven and arrange asparagus alongside eggs. Scatter the prosciutto over and sprinkle with cheese. Return to oven and continue baking 1 minute longer, or until cheese melts.
Makes 4 servings

Whole Egg Entrees

POACHED EGGS

An attractive poached egg has a well-centered yolk surrounded by a trim, neat white cooked to your desired firmness. For best results use very fresh eggs, preferably not more than a few days old. The whites of fresh eggs hold together, whereas older eggs will form a raggedy-edged white as they cook in a liquid. To compensate for using regular market eggs, a new technique calls for heat-treating the eggs before poaching. To do this, immerse each egg, still in the shell, in enough rapidly boiling water to cover, and remove the egg in exactly 8 seconds. Don't worry if eggs crack. Use at once or refrigerate for no more than 2 days. If you have wonderfully fresh eggs this step is not necessary.

If you do not heat-treat the eggs, there are other techniques for achieving firmly edged, neat whites. One is to swirl the poaching liquid with a fork until a whirlpool appears in the center. Stop stirring, and when the water is moving quite slowly, slide an egg into the center. The white will wrap around the yolk making a neat round. Another technique is to place buttered canning jar rings in the water or use tuna or cat food cans with both the top and bottom lids removed. Slide the eggs into the jar rings or can rings and cook until desired doneness. Remove rings with tongs, then lift out eggs.

To poach heat-treated eggs or plain fresh eggs, first fill a pan with enough water to cover an egg by about 1 inch. You need a large wide pan if you intend to poach more than one egg at a time. Add 1 tablespoon white vinegar for each quart of water and a little salt to help eggs keep their shape. Heat water until a few bubbles break on the surface, reduce heat until bubbles just form on the pan bottom, and break each egg directly into the water, holding it as close to the surface as is comfortably possible. Do not crowd eggs in pan, and do not allow the water to get hot enough to jiggle the eggs as it will tear them apart. Cook until eggs are set to your liking, about 3 to 5 minutes for soft yolks and firm whites. Test by pressing the egg gently with a spoon to check the firmness. Remove eggs with a slotted spoon. If you are poaching a quantity of eggs, use fresh water each time for the best looking eggs.

You can pre-poach eggs and store them in a container in cold water; cover and refrigerate up to 2 days. Serve cold or reheat by immersing in a generous amount of water that is just hot to the touch. Let stand 5 to 10 minutes to heat through, then drain and serve.

Variations

• Arrange poached eggs on a bed of flaked crab meat, spoon over Mornay Sauce (page 62) and sprinkle with grated Parmesan cheese. Brown quickly under a hot broiler.

• Arrange in individual ramekins a few slices of hot cooked chicken breast meat or turkey, hot steamed broccoli flowerets and a poached egg. Spoon Hollandaise Sauce (page 118) over.

• Sauté a chopped onion in butter in a large frying pan, add corned beef hash and heat through. Make several depressions on top and place hot poached eggs in each depression.

• Nestle a hot poached egg in large mushroom caps or artichoke bottoms which have first been sautéed in butter. Spoon Hollandaise Sauce (page 118) over.

• Sauté rounds of firm white bread without crusts in butter until golden, place a poached egg on top of each and cover with Mornay Sauce (page 62) and grated Swiss cheese. Slip under the broiler until the sauce is lightly browned. If desired, mix a little sautéed sliced mushrooms and minced ham or small cooked shrimp with part of the sauce and spread over each bread round as a bed for the egg.

EGGS BENEDICT

This classic brunch dish is delightful accompanied by artichokes vinaigrette or freshly cooked asparagus spears. You might finish off with strawberries steeped in wine.

6 split and buttered English muffins
6 slices cooked ham
6 poached eggs, kept warm
Hollandaise Sauce, page 118

Toast English muffins until golden brown and arrange cut-side up on a serving platter or individual plates. Cover one half of each muffin with a ham slice and poached egg. Top with Hollandaise Sauce.
Makes 6 servings

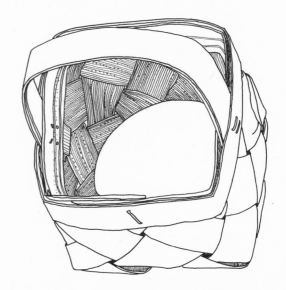

Whole Egg Entrees

FRENCHMAN'S HASH

Leftover beef roast is the starting point for this butter-browned, family-style hash.

1 medium-sized onion, chopped
4 tablespoons butter
1-1/2 cups diced cooked potatoes
2-1/2 cups diced cooked roast beef
1/4 pound mushrooms, sliced (approximately 1 cup)
salt and pepper to taste
1/3 cup heavy cream
4 eggs
1/2 cup cherry tomatoes, halved
3 tablespoons chopped parsley

Using a large frying pan, sauté onion in butter until golden. Add potatoes and beef and cook until browned. Add mushrooms and sauté just until glazed. Season with salt and pepper. Pour cream into pan and cook until hash is crusty underneath. Meanwhile poach or fry the eggs and place them on the hash. Ring pan with tomatoes and sprinkle with parsley.
Makes 4 servings

EGGS FLORENTINE

Individual ramekins or baking dishes make festive containers for presenting this luncheon dish.

1-1/2 pounds spinach, chopped, cooked and kept warm
salt and pepper to taste
freshly grated nutmeg
8 poached eggs, kept warm
Mornay Sauce, following
freshly grated Parmesan or Romano cheese

Season spinach with salt and pepper. Butter ramekins or individual baking dishes large enough to hold 2 eggs and spread a layer of spinach in each. Sprinkle with grated nutmeg. Nestle 2 poached eggs in each. Cover with Mornay Sauce. Dust with grated Parmesan. Place under the broiler until nicely browned.
Makes 4 servings

MORNAY SAUCE

In a saucepan, make a roux with 2 tablespoons each butter and flour. Slowly add 1 cup heated milk and cook and stir until thickened. Add salt and white pepper to taste. Beat together 1 egg yolk and 2 tablespoons half-and-half. Add a little sauce to egg mixture, stir to blend, then return to saucepan and cook until heated through. Stir in 2 tablespoons each grated Parmesan cheese and grated Swiss or Gruyère cheese; remove from heat. Makes 1-1/2 cups.

MEXICAN EGGS

Here is a brunch dish to join hot rolled flour tortillas and fresh melon or pineapple.

4 slices bacon, diced
1 medium-sized onion, finely chopped
6 to 8 medium-sized ripe tomatoes, peeled and chopped, or
1 28-ounce can tomatoes with juice
2 tablespoons Ortega's chile salsa
1 clove garlic, minced
1/2 teaspoon each crumbled dried oregano and ground cumin
salt and pepper to taste
1 teaspoon sugar
1/2 cup shredded Monterey Jack cheese
6 eggs
finely chopped fresh coriander

Using a large frying pan, sauté bacon until almost crisp; drain off most of the drippings. Add onion to pan and sauté until golden. Add tomatoes and juice, salsa, garlic, oregano, cumin, salt, pepper and sugar, stirring to break up tomatoes. Simmer uncovered until sauce is thick, about 15 minutes. Add cheese and heat until melted. Break eggs into sauce, cover pan and cook until set. Garnish with coriander.
Makes 6 servings

AVOCADO AND EGG TOSTADAS

Mexican-style tostadas are a festive choice for a Sunday brunch or late supper.

4 flour tortillas, about 6 inches in diameter
2 cups shredded Monterey Jack or Cheddar cheese
1/4 cup finely chopped canned green chiles
1-1/2 cups shredded iceberg lettuce
2 green onions, chopped
4 poached eggs, kept warm
1 avocado
1/2 cup cherry tomatoes, halved
pitted ripe olives for garnish

Sprinkle tortillas with cheese and chiles. Place on a baking sheet and bake in a 400° oven for about 5 minutes or until cheese is melted. Remove from oven and place each tortilla on a dinner plate cheese side up. Sprinkle each one with lettuce and green onions. Top each with a hot poached egg. Peel and slice avocado and arrange 2 or 3 slices on each tostada. Garnish with cherry tomatoes and ripe olives.
Makes 4 servings

Scrambled Eggs
Omelets
Frittatas

Scrambled Eggs, Omelets & Frittatas

SCRAMBLED EGGS

You don't need ultra-fresh eggs for scrambling as you aren't concerned with keeping the egg shape. You do wish to create a velvety-textured egg mixture. A small amount of liquid, about 1 teaspoon to 1 tablespoon per egg, will give a more tender "bite" to the product. You may add water, milk, heavy cream, sour cream or wine. Figure on 2 eggs per serving. Mix the liquid thoroughly with the eggs using a fork or whisk. Heat the pan over moderate heat and add butter or margarine to a depth of about 1/8 inch. When butter stops foaming, pour in the eggs. As soon as an opaque layer forms within a few seconds on the pan bottom, push it to one side with a wide spatula, allowing the liquid egg to flow underneath. Continue stirring until cooked through without allowing it to brown. The scrambled eggs should have a moist look on the surface.

Some cooks prefer no liquid in their scrambled eggs. Instead they stir in a little butter or heavy cream at the end of scrambling, or blend in a whole raw egg.

Variations
• Mix in 1 or 2 tablespoons grated Swiss or Gruyère cheese at the end.
• Mix in 1 teaspoon minced fresh herbs such as parsley, chives or tarragon at the beginning and scatter over more herbs at the end.
• Serve eggs on a platter surrounded by fresh cooked asparagus spears and rolls of smoked salmon.
• Add drained, chopped oysters to the eggs just as they start to set. Serve on toasted English muffins.
• Garnish scrambled eggs with browned pork sausages, crisp bacon strips, sautéed chicken livers or grilled ham or Canadian bacon.
• Season scrambled eggs with diced green chile pepper and grated Monterey Jack cheese. Roll up in a heated flour tortilla.

Scrambled Eggs, Omelets & Frittatas

MEXICAN-STYLE SCRAMBLED EGGS

Sour cream, parsley and sautéed onions lend a pleasing change of pace to scrambled eggs.

1 bunch green onions (approximately 6), chopped (white part only), or
1 small yellow onion, chopped
3 tablespoons butter
8 eggs
1/3 cup sour cream
1/4 cup chopped fresh coriander or parsley
salt and freshly ground pepper to taste
1 avocado, peeled and sliced
1 tomato, cut in wedges
coriander or parsley sprigs

Using a large frying pan, sauté onions in butter until glazed. Beat eggs until blended and mix in sour cream, chopped coriander, salt and pepper. Pour eggs into the onion mixture and cook over medium heat, stirring gently until set but still creamy. Serve garnished with avocado, tomato and coriander sprigs.
Makes 4 servings

PIPÉRADE

The Basque way of scrambling eggs results in a colorful, zestful dish.

2 large onions, thinly sliced
3 tablespoons bacon fat
3 red or green bell peppers, seeded and sliced in julienne
salt and pepper to taste
1/4 teaspoon crumbled dried marjoram
4 large tomatoes, peeled and chopped
6 eggs
6 slices sourdough French bread, spread with garlic butter and toasted

Using a large frying pan, sauté onions in bacon fat until glazed. Add peppers, salt, pepper and marjoram and cook until peppers are soft. Add tomatoes and simmer 5 to 10 minutes longer for flavors to blend. Beat eggs until blended, pour over vegetables and stir gently until set. Accompany with garlic-buttered French bread.
Makes 6 servings

Scrambled Eggs, Omelets & Frittatas

OMELETS

The word "omelet" is used loosely to cover a range of beaten-egg dishes cooked in a pan. Traditionally it refers to a French-style omelet which is tender and firm outside and soft and creamy within. It may be rolled or folded and filled with a wide variety of fillings.

A soufflé omelet, sometimes called a fluffy omelet, is a style of omelet in which the yolks and whites are beaten separately, flavorings are added, and the whole is first heated over the cook-top and then oven-baked until browned.

The Italian frittata and Chinese egg foo yung are both types of omelets, but the beaten eggs and other ingredients are cooked like a pancake, undisturbed until set.

To cook a French-style omelet, first you must select a proper pan. You have a choice of stainless steel, plain or treated aluminum, or plain or enameled iron. I prefer a French-type plain iron pan with sloping sides and a long handle. A pan with a bottom diameter of 7 inches is the right size for a 2- or 3-egg omelet.

Treat the pan before you use it. First scrub it with steel wool and rinse it. Heat the pan until hot to the touch and then rub it with cooking oil and let it stand overnight. Before making your first omelet, sprinkle a light coating of table salt over it, heat it and rub it with paper toweling; discard salt and rub the pan clean. Use the pan only for omelets and merely wipe it out with a paper towel after each use. If you should need to clean it, heat it, sprinkle it with salt and rub clean.

If you are making a quantity of omelets, you may beat the necessary number of eggs and the seasonings together in a bowl and use a ladle or measuring cup to pour out the right amount. Two large eggs measure about 6 tablespoons. If you are preparing several omelets in succession, keep them warm in a low oven. A battery of omelets, such as a half dozen or a dozen, are quick to make as each one takes about 30 seconds to cook. Serve as soon as possible.

Scrambled Eggs, Omelets & Frittatas

CLASSIC OMELET

This basic omelet can be filled in countless ways.

2 eggs
1 teaspoon water
1/8 teaspoon salt
dash pepper
2 teaspoons butter

Beat together lightly the eggs, water, salt and pepper. Heat a 7-inch omelet pan, add butter, and when it stops foaming, tilt pan to coat evenly. Add eggs all at once. Shake the pan, slip a thin spatula under the eggs just as soon as they are set and lift, tilting the pan to let the uncooked portion flow underneath. Fill, if desired, then fold over and turn out of pan onto a hot plate.
Makes 1 omelet

Fillings
• Shredded Monterey Jack cheese and chopped green chile peppers
• Major Grey's chutney, chopped, and slivered toasted almonds or cashews
• Mixed minced fresh herbs such as tarragon, parsley, chives and marjoram
• Caviar and sour cream
• Smoked salmon, sour cream and chopped green onions
• Sautéed mushrooms and sour cream
• Crab meat or shrimp, quickly heated in butter
• Shredded Gruyère cheese
• Cooked asparagus tips and sour cream
• Sautéed chopped spinach and chopped green onions
• Cooked diced artichoke hearts and Parmesan cheese
• Sliced avocado and shredded Monterey Jack cheese, with alfalfa sprouts if desired
• Sautéed chicken livers and mushrooms or green onions

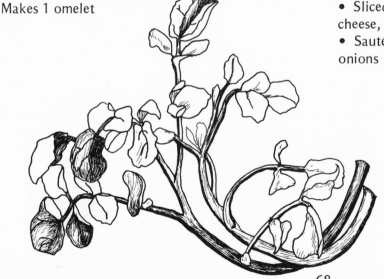

Scrambled Eggs, Omelets & Frittatas

HAM AND EGG OVEN OMELET

This oven omelet makes a congenial brunch dish for a Sunday morning. Accompany with flaky croissants and a fresh-fruit platter of sliced oranges, pineapple and berries.

8 eggs
1 cup milk
1/2 teaspoon salt
1/4 teaspoon ground nutmeg
1/2 cup julienne-cut cooked ham
2 cups shredded Swiss cheese
3/4 cup sourdough French bread cubes
2 tablespoons butter, melted

Beat eggs until blended and mix in milk, salt, nutmeg, ham and cheese. Pour egg mixture into a buttered ovenproof baking dish about 9-1/2 inches in diameter. Roll bread cubes in melted butter to coat and scatter over the top. Bake in a 350° oven for 35 to 40 minutes, or until golden brown and puffed. Serve at once, cut in wedges.
Makes 6 servings

ITALIAN RICE OMELET

Here is a fine way to utilize leftover rice for a fast luncheon or supper entrée.

6 eggs
salt and pepper to taste
2 tablespoons butter
3/4 cup hot cooked long-grain rice
1/2 cup diced Gruyère cheese
2 ounces salami, cut in slivers
2 green onions, chopped

Beat eggs until blended and mix in salt and pepper. Melt butter in a large frying pan and pour in eggs. Shake the pan, slip a thin spatula under the eggs just as soon as they begin to set and lift, tilting the pan to let the uncooked portion flow underneath. When eggs are almost set, spoon rice, cheese, salami and onions down the center of the omelet and fold over. Cook over very low heat until filling is heated through.
Makes 3 to 4 servings

Scrambled Eggs, Omelets & Frittatas

SOUFFLÉ OMELET BON LABOUREUR

A French country inn located at Chenonceaux makes a specialty of this herb-scented souffléed omelet. It resembles a balloon-sized blimp as it arrives on the diner's table.

6 eggs, separated
1/2 teaspoon salt
1 teaspoon each chopped fresh parsley, chives
  and tarragon
2 tablespoons butter

Beat egg whites with salt until soft peaks form. Beat yolks until thick and lemon colored. Mix herbs into yolks and fold into the whites. Heat a flameproof 1-1/2-quart oval baking dish or pan with butter and spoon in the soufflé. Cook over medium heat until set underneath, about 3 to 4 minutes. Then bake in a 350° oven for 5 minutes or until omelet is set through and the top is golden. Serve at once.
Makes 4 to 6 servings

Note The French chef evidently browns the soufflé in a frying pan and then transfers it to a baking platter for final baking. Thus a rounded look is achieved.

GERMAN BACON AND POTATO OMELET

The hearty German omelet, rhythmically called *Hoppelpoppel*, furnishes a good last-minute supper entrée. Accompany with black rye bread, a creamy coleslaw, and apple strudel or fresh fruit and cheese for dessert.

2 medium-sized boiling potatoes
6 slices bacon, diced
1 small onion, finely chopped
4 eggs
1 tablespoon half-and-half
2 tablespoons chopped parsley
salt and freshly ground pepper to taste

Cook whole, unpeeled potatoes in boiling salted water until barely tender. Drain, peel and slice about 1/4 inch thick. While the potatoes are cooking, sauté bacon until crispy in a large frying pan; transfer bacon to paper towels to drain and pour off all but 2 tablespoons of the bacon drippings. Add onion and sliced potatoes to the frying pan and sauté until onion is glazed. Beat eggs until blended. Mix half-and-half, parsley, salt and pepper into the eggs and pour over the potato mixture. Sprinkle with cooked bacon. Cook until the eggs are set, shaking pan to prevent them from sticking.
Makes 4 servings

FILBERT AND GRUYÈRE OMELET

For a spur-of-the-moment luncheon or supper entrée, here is a festive open-face omelet that goes together fast with ingredients generally on hand.

4 slices bacon, diced
1/2 cup filberts, halved or coarsely chopped
1 small onion, finely chopped
2 tablespoons butter
6 eggs
3/4 cup shredded Gruyère or Jarlsberg cheese
2 tablespoons minced parsley
1/2 cup each plain yogurt and sour cream

Cook bacon over medium heat until crisp and browned. Remove bacon from pan and set aside. Drain off all but 2 tablespoons of the bacon drippings. Add nuts to pan and sauté until browned; remove from pan. Sauté onion in remaining drippings until glazed; set aside.

In a clean 10- or 11-inch frying pan, melt butter over moderately high heat. Beat eggs until light and pour in pan, pushing them from the bottom as they set and allowing the uncooked portion to flow underneath. When the top of the omelet is almost set, sprinkle with cheese, onion, bacon and parsley. Mix together the yogurt and sour cream, and spoon into the center. Ring with toasted filberts. Cut into wedges to serve.
Makes 4 to 6 servings

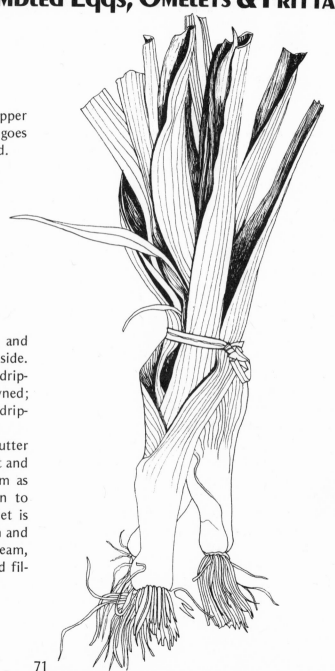

Scrambled Eggs, Omelets & Frittatas

BASIC FRITTATA, MUSHROOM STYLE

The Italian-style omelet, called frittata, acquires a nut-like flavored, golden crust as it is fried in olive oil, much like a pancake. Frittatas are delicious cold as well as hot. They may be cut into small bites for an appetizer.

1/2 pound mushrooms, thinly sliced
  (approximately 2 cups)
2 shallots or green onions, chopped
3 tablespoons olive oil or butter
6 eggs
salt and pepper to taste
1/2 teaspoon crumbled dried tarragon
3 tablespoons chopped parsley
1/3 cup freshly shredded Romano or Parmesan
  cheese

Using a large frying pan, sauté mushrooms and shallots in oil just until glazed. Beat eggs and mix in salt, pepper, tarragon, parsley and half of the cheese. Pour in the egg mixture and cook over medium-high heat without stirring until the edges are lightly browned. Sprinkle with remaining cheese and slip under the broiler to brown the top lightly. Cut into wedges to serve.
Makes 4 to 6 servings

Artichoke Frittata Substitute for the mushrooms, 1 8-ounce package frozen artichoke hearts, cooked in boiling salted water until tender, about 7 min-utes, and drained. Use crumbled dried basil or marjoram in place of the tarragon and continue as in Basic Frittata, above.

Spinach Frittata Substitute for the mushrooms, 3/4 pound spinach, finely chopped, and 1 clove garlic, minced. Sauté in oil just until heated through. Omit tarragon. Continue as in Basic Frittata, above.

Meat or Seafood Frittata Substitute for the mushrooms, 1-1/2 cups julienne-cut baked ham, cooked tongue or chicken, or 1-1/2 cups small cooked shrimp or crab meat. Sauté shallots until glazed, add meat and sauté just until heated through. Continue as in Basic Frittata, above.

Mexican Frittata Substitute for the mushrooms, 1-1/2 cups diced cooked chicken. Sauté shallots until glazed; add chicken and sauté just until heated through. Omit tarragon and add 3 tablespoons chopped green chile peppers and 1/2 cup sliced ripe olives to the eggs. Substitute fresh coriander for the parsley, if desired. Continue as in Basic Frittata, above.

Croûton and Bacon Frittata Omit mushrooms, shallots and tarragon. Stir 3/4 cup garlic-flavored sourdough bread croûtons and 1/2 cup crumbled crisply cooked bacon into the eggs. Continue as in Basic Frittata, above.

SHREDDED ZUCCHINI PANCAKE

You may cook a variety of vegetables—red or green bell peppers, mushrooms, spinach, leeks or bean sprouts—in an egg pancake as a simple luncheon or first-course dish. Sour cream dressed with chives makes a fine companion.

3 zucchini (approximately 1 pound)
1/2 teaspoon salt
2 tablespoons olive oil
1 shallot, finely chopped
1/2 teaspoon crumbled dried tarragon
1 clove garlic, minced
2 eggs, lightly beaten

Trim ends from the zucchini and shred them. Sprinkle with salt and let stand 15 minutes for the moisture to exude. Then squeeze or wring with a towel to dry. Heat oil in a 10-inch frying pan; add zucchini, shallot, tarragon and garlic, and sauté until zucchini is crisp-tender. Pour in egg and cook until set. Flip the pancake and cook the other side for a few seconds. Turn out and cut in wedges.
Makes 4 luncheon entrées or first-course servings

Pepper Pancake Omit zucchini. Halve 2 large red or green bell peppers and remove seeds and stem. Cut into 1/2-inch chunks. Sauté in oil with remaining ingredients as directed above.

Mushroom Pancake Omit zucchini. Wash and then thinly slice or chop 1/4 pound mushrooms. Sauté in oil with remaining ingredients as directed above.

Spinach Pancake Omit zucchini. Wash 1 small bunch spinach (approximately 12 ounces) and remove stems. Chop leaves coarsely. Sauté in oil, substituting 1/2 teaspoon crumbled dried marjoram for tarragon. Continue as directed above.

Leek Pancake Omit zucchini. Thoroughly wash 2 or 3 leeks and trim ends. Slice thinly the white part and 2 inches of the green part. Sauté in oil as directed above.

Bean Sprouts Pancake Omit zucchini. Trim ends from 2 green onions and thinly slice. Wash 1-1/2 cups bean sprouts. Sauté onions and bean sprouts in oil with remaining ingredients as directed above.

Scrambled Eggs, Omelets & Frittatas

EGG FOO YUNG

Golden brown egg pancakes, flecked with colorful vegetables, are a fast and economical supper entrée or a pleasant addition to an Oriental meal.

3 eggs
1/2 teaspoon salt
1/2 cup bean sprouts
1/3 pound green peas, shelled, or
1/3 cup frozen peas, thawed
4 mushrooms, thinly sliced
1 8-ounce can minced clams, drained, or
1/4 pound cooked ground pork
peanut oil as needed
3/4 cup chicken stock
1 tablespoon soy sauce
1 tablespoon cornstarch, dissolved in
2 tablespoons cold water

Beat eggs and 1/4 teaspoon of the salt until blended and mix in bean sprouts, peas, mushrooms and clams or cooked pork. Heat 2 tablespoons of the oil in a large frying pan over moderately high heat and add 1/4 cup of the egg mixture at a time for each pancake. Cook until golden brown on the bottom, about 1 minute, then turn and cook on the other side until golden. Repeat with remaining batter, adding oil to the pan as needed. Meanwhile bring stock to a boil and add soy sauce, the remaining 1/4 teaspoon of salt and the cornstarch mixture. Cook, stirring until thickened. Serve pancakes and pass sauce to spoon over them.
Makes 8 pancakes, or 4 servings

STIRRED EGGS AND PORK

This stir-fry dish is a pleasant addition to an Oriental dinner. Alone, it makes a fast luncheon entrée to accompany with pears or grapes.

1/2 pound boneless lean pork butt
1 tablespoon soy sauce
2 tablespoons peanut oil
2 green onions, chopped
1/4 pound small button mushrooms
4 eggs

Slice pork paper-thin and toss with soy sauce. Heat oil in a large frying pan or wok and stir-fry pork until brown, about 2 minutes. Add onions and stir-fry 1 minute. Add mushrooms and stir-fry just until glazed. Beat eggs and pour in, stirring gently until set. Serve at once.
Makes 4 servings

Souffles

Souffles

SOUFFLÉS

A soufflé is made by combining a thick egg yolk-base sauce with stiffly beaten egg whites. It is turned into an ovenproof dish or pan and baked until puffed and browned. The word soufflé stems from *souffler,* meaning to breathe, puff up or inflate. Unfortunately it also falls when allowed to cool. Soufflés may be savory or sweet, with flavorings varying from cheese, seafood and puréed vegetables, to chocolate, praline and liqueur.

Soufflés are actually easy to master and have more flexibility in their timing than many cooks imagine. Most soufflés can be completely assembled and allowed to wait on the counter at room temperature, lightly covered with a lid, for up to an hour. Once the soufflé is baked and if the guests are not yet ready for it, turn off the oven and let it wait there. It will stand tall, without collapsing, for 10 minutes or longer.

The lightness of a soufflé depends largely on how properly the egg whites are beaten and how lightly they are folded into the sauce base. Start with egg whites at room temperature. (If they are cold from the refrigerator, place their container in a bowl of warm water to warm gently.) Be certain the bowl and beater are free from oily film and that the whites do not contain a speck of egg yolk.

A small amount of acid helps stabilize beaten egg whites. This is why French chefs prefer an unlined copper bowl, as the acidity of the copper acts as a stabilizer. Without this aid, beat the whites until foamy and then beat in about 1/4 teaspoon cream of tartar for every 4 egg whites.

The big balloon French whip is preferred by many authorities for achieving the greatest volume. Nonetheless, an electric beater will certainly do; those with a balloon-type whip attachment provide an advantage. Beat the whites until stiff but not dry—to the point where they rise to glossy mounds, look "wet," and are firm enough to stand in upright peaks when the whip or beater is lifted. If whipped to the dry stage, they become granular and break up when folded into the main mixture, and the soufflé does not rise to its greatest height when baked. If you accidently do overbeat the whites, add another egg white and beat again. The sheen will return. Use your beaten egg whites at once. Beaten whites left to stand will settle out into a liquid at the bottom. If they can't be used immediately, add another egg white and beat again just before using them.

Folding means to incorporate a fragile mixture, such as beaten egg whites, very gently into a heavier mixture, such as the soufflé base. The point is to retain the air already beaten into the whites.

First stir a big spoonful (about one-fourth) of the beaten whites into the soufflé base to lighten it. Then with a rubber scraper, scoop the rest of the egg whites on top. Fold in by cutting the scraper down from the center to the bottom of the pan or bowl, then run it along the bottom toward you and against the edge of the pan lifting up the sauce and turning it on top of the whites, rotating the pan as you work. Continue until all the egg white is blended in, taking about 1 minute, although it is better to leave a few unblended specks than to be too thorough.

A soufflé may be baked in a wide range of containers. A straight-sided soufflé dish is traditional, but certainly not essential. You may use a charlotte mold, fondue pot, ovenproof casserole or a large elegant copper frying pan or gratin pan. A large shallow pan offers lots of surface to give crustiness to the soufflé. Plan to butter the bottom and sides of the mold or pan. (Some cooks prefer leaving a glass or porcelain dish ungreased.) You may then coat the mold with grated cheese for a savory souffle or granulated sugar for a dessert soufflé. To coat, spoon in a few tablespoons of the coating ingredient into the mold. Then holding the mold in your hands, roll it around and around so that sides and bottom are evenly but lightly coated. Turn it upside down and give it a bang to empty out any surplus coating.

For a soufflé to look quite spectacular, it is desirable to serve it well risen. To achieve this, it needs a foil collar to support it during baking. If a soufflé is baked in a more open flat dish, a collar is not necessary. To make a foil collar, fold a 12-inch wide sheet of foil cut 4 inches longer than the circumference of the soufflé dish in half lengthwise. With the fold as the top of the collar, butter the upper half of one side lightly. Place the foil collar with buttered side facing inward around the outside of the top of the dish, letting it extend 2-1/2 inches above the rim. Then double-fold the ends to seal in place.

To make a soufflé with a "crown," run a knife or spoon around the top of the soufflé making a cut about 1-1/2 inches deep and about 1 inch from the edge of the dish. This will give a striking "high-hat" appearance to the soufflé.

Place the soufflé on a rack in the middle level of a preheated oven. The French, among others, prefer to serve soufflés when the center is still soft. At this point, the top of the soufflé should ripple in the center only when the dish is gently moved. When served, the soft custardy center becomes a sauce for the remaining soufflé. Another style is to cook the soufflé evenly throughout. To test, touch the top of the soufflé with a finger; it should feel set. Serve a soufflé using a large serving spoon and fork held vertically.

Souffles

BASIC VEGETABLE SOUFFLÉ, SPINACH VERSION

The usual method is to thicken a savory soufflé with a béchamel sauce. Here a cornstarch-thickened sauce results in a lighter soufflé with fewer calories.

1 cup milk
3 tablespoons cornstarch, blended with
3 tablespoons water
3/4 teaspoon salt
1/4 teaspoon ground nutmeg
1 small onion, finely chopped
2 teaspoons butter
1 large bunch spinach (approximately 1 pound),
   finely chopped
6 eggs, separated
3/4 cup grated Swiss or Gruyère cheese

Heat milk in a saucepan until scalded; add cornstarch mixture and stir over heat until thickened. Stir in salt and nutmeg and set aside. Sauté onion in butter until glazed. Add spinach and cook until heated through (still slightly crisp); drain off any liquid. Place spinach and egg yolks in a blender container and purée until spinach is finely minced. Stir spinach mixture into the cornstarch-thickened sauce. Mix in all but 2 tablespoons of the cheese. Beat egg whites until stiff but not dry and fold in. Butter a 2-quart soufflé dish with a foil collar, coat lightly with remaining 2 tablespoons of cheese and turn soufflé into dish. Bake in a 375° oven for 35 minutes or until puffed and golden brown.
Makes 6 to 8 servings

Broccoli Soufflé Substitute 1-1/2 cups cooked chopped broccoli for the spinach, puréeing it with the sautéed onions and egg yolks. Proceed as directed above.

Mushroom Soufflé Substitute 1-1/2 cups (approximately 6 ounces) finely chopped mushrooms for the spinach, sautéing them in butter with the onion until glazed. Purée with egg yolks and proceed as directed above.

Asparagus Tips Soufflé Substitute 1-1/2 cups cooked diced asparagus tips for the spinach, puréeing them with the onions and egg yolks. Proceed as directed above.

FANTASTIC WHOLE-EGG CHEESE SOUFFLÉ

This super-fast soufflé is made with whole eggs. There's no need to separate them at all. The result is meltingly rich and creamy. For a large party, the recipe may be doubled or tripled.

6 eggs
1 cup heavy cream
1 teaspoon salt
freshly ground pepper to taste
1/4 teaspoon ground nutmeg
1-1/2 cups grated Cheddar or Swiss cheese
1/2 cup grated Parmesan cheese

Beat eggs until thick and light and mix in cream, salt, pepper and nutmeg, beating well. Fold in the cheeses. Pour into a well-buttered 1-1/2-quart baking dish or an ovenproof 10-1/2-inch frying pan. Bake in a 425° oven for 30 to 35 minutes or until set through.
Makes 6 servings

SOUTHERN SPOON BREAD SOUFFLÉ

This soufflé-like hot bread is a choice Southern accompaniment to ham, roast pork or barbecued chicken.

2-1/4 cups milk
3/4 cup yellow cornmeal
2 tablespoons sugar
1 teaspoon salt
4 tablespoons butter
4 eggs, separated

Heat milk just to boiling and gradually stir in cornmeal. Lower heat and cook until cornmeal is thickened, about 10 minutes. Stir in sugar, salt and butter, and remove from heat. Beat egg yolks until light and stir in the hot cornmeal mixture. Beat egg whites until stiff and fold into cornmeal mixture. Turn into a buttered 1-1/2-quart casserole. Bake in a 375° oven for 35 minutes or until set and golden.
Makes 6 to 8 servings

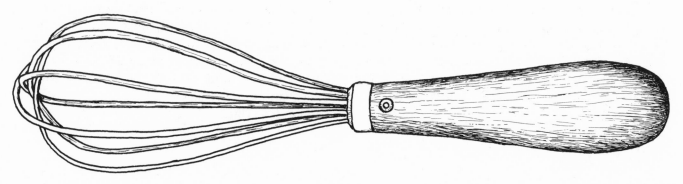

Souffles

CHEDDAR SOUFFLÉ WITH GARLIC NUGGETS

Butter-crisped sourdough croûtons spark this cheese-enriched soufflé. Italian sausages, poached in red wine, are a splendid companion.

2 slices sourdough French bread, cut in cubes
4 tablespoons butter
1 clove garlic, minced
1/4 cup all-purpose flour
1/2 teaspoon each salt and dry mustard
1/4 teaspoon ground nutmeg
1 cup milk, heated
6 eggs, separated
1-1/4 cups grated Cheddar cheese
1/4 teaspoon cream of tartar

Sauté bread cubes in 1 tablespoon of the butter with garlic until golden; set aside. Melt remaining butter in a saucepan and stir in flour, salt, mustard and nutmeg; cook and stir 2 minutes. Gradually stir in milk and, stirring constantly, cook until thickened. Remove from heat and mix in egg yolks and cheese. Beat egg whites until foamy, add cream of tartar and beat until soft peaks form. Fold into the cheese sauce. Fold in garlic croûtons. Spoon into a buttered 2-quart soufflé dish with a foil collar. Bake in a 375° oven for 30 to 35 minutes or until set.
Makes 6 servings

SHRIMP AND CHEESE CUSTARD SOUFFLÉ

Here is a "mock" soufflé that you can assemble as long as a day ahead and bake at the last minute. Custard-soaked bread and grated Swiss cheese provide the air lift.

6 slices firm white bread, crusts removed
4 tablespoons butter, melted
1 cup grated Swiss cheese
1 green onion, chopped
2 tablespoons chopped parsley
1/4 to 1/2 pound small fresh cooked shrimp
3 eggs
1/2 teaspoon each salt and Dijon-style mustard
1-1/2 cups milk
1/2 cup sour cream

Cut each slice of bread in half diagonally. Dip in melted butter and arrange half of bread in a 7- or 8-inch square baking dish. Sprinkle with half each of the cheese, onion, parsley and shrimp. Cover, making layers, with the remaining bread, cheese, onion, parsley and shrimp. Beat eggs until blended and mix in salt, mustard, milk and sour cream. Pour egg mixture over layers. Cover and chill 2 hours or overnight. Bake in a 350° oven for 30 to 40 minutes or until puffed and golden brown. Cut in squares or rectangles.
Makes 6 servings

SHRIMP AND TURBOT SOUFFLÉ

This festive light seafood soufflé is ideal for a guest luncheon or light dinner. Accompany with fresh asparagus spears and a citrus and avocado salad.

2/3 pound turbot or sole fillets
1 cup milk
2-1/2 tablespoons cornstarch, blended with
2-1/2 tablespoons water
1/2 teaspoon each salt and dry mustard
1/4 teaspoon ground nutmeg and freshly
   ground pepper
dash Tabasco sauce
5 eggs, separated
2/3 cup grated Gruyère or Jarlsberg cheese
1 shallot, minced
1/3 pound small fresh cooked shrimp
2 teaspoons butter
1 tablespoon dry sherry

Cut turbot into 1-inch pieces and place in a blender container with 1/3 of the milk; purée until smooth. Heat remaining milk until scalded and stir in the cornstarch mixture; stirring, cook until thickened. Season with salt, mustard, nutmeg, pepper and Tabasco. Add fish purée and cook 2 minutes, stirring. Mix in egg yolks and half the cheese. Sauté shallot and shrimp in butter, add sherry and cook down until juices evaporate. Beat egg whites until stiff but not dry and fold into the yolk mixture. Spoon half of the soufflé into a buttered 2-quart casserole. Scatter over half of the shrimp. Cover with remaining soufflé and sprinkle over remaining shrimp and cheese. Bake in a 375° oven for 30 minutes or until puffed and golden brown.
Makes 6 servings

Souffles

SOUFFLÉ-TOPPED SOLE

Flaked sole is masked in a puffy soufflé in this handsome platter-sized presentation.

3/4 pound sole fillets
1/2 cup dry white wine
1/2 teaspoon each salt and crumbled dried tarragon
2 green onions, chopped
2 tablespoons butter
3 tablespoons flour
1 cup milk, heated
1/2 teaspoon salt
dash pepper
2 eggs, separated
1/2 cup grated Parmesan cheese
4 egg whites
1/2 cup sour cream

Place sole, wine, salt, tarragon and 1 chopped green onion in a frying pan. Cover and simmer for 8 to 10 minutes, or until fish flakes easily with a fork. Lift out fish to a large buttered ovenproof platter, reserving liquid. Separate it into 1-inch pieces. Cook down the poaching liquid until reduced to 2 tablespoons; reserve.

Melt butter, blend in flour and cook and stir 2 minutes. Gradually stir in milk, salt and pepper and cook, stirring until thickened. Remove from heat and mix in the reduced fish stock, egg yolks and half the cheese. Beat egg whites until stiff but not dry, fold into yolk mixture and spoon over the fish. Sprinkle top with remaining cheese. Bake in a 425° oven for about 15 to 20 minutes or until puffed and golden brown. Blend remaining green onion with sour cream; serve as sauce alongside.
Makes 4 servings

SALMON SOUFFLÉ ROULADE

These handsome pinwheels are made of a savory soufflé spread with a smoked salmon and sour cream filling, and can serve as a party luncheon entrée or a first course.

4 tablespoons butter
1/2 cup all-purpose flour
2 cups milk, heated
1/2 teaspoon salt
1 tablespoon brandy or sherry
4 eggs, separated
1 cup (1/2 pint) sour cream
3 ounces smoked salmon, diced
1/2 teaspoon grated lemon peel
2 green onions, chopped
cherry tomatoes for garnish

Melt butter in a saucepan and blend in flour; cook and stir 2 minutes. Remove from heat and gradually stir in milk, blending with a wire whisk. Return to heat and cook and stir until thickened. Remove from heat and stir in salt, brandy and egg yolks. Beat egg whites until stiff and fold into yolk mixture. Butter a 10- by 15-inch jelly-roll pan, line with waxed paper and butter waxed paper. Spoon in batter and spread evenly into pan. Bake in a 350° oven for 35 minutes or until golden brown and top springs back when touched lightly. Turn pan upside down on a rack, remove pan and peel off paper. Mix together sour cream, salmon, lemon peel and onions and spread over the soufflé. Roll up from a lengthwise side, place on a serving platter and garnish with cherry tomatoes. Slice 1-1/4 inches thick to serve.
Makes 6 to 8 servings

SALMON SOUFFLÉ AUBERGE DE L'ILL

A golden soufflé masks salmon fillets in the manner of a great French auberge in Illhaeusern.

1/2 pound turbot fillets
2 eggs, separated
1/2 teaspoon salt
1-1/2 pounds salmon fillets
1/3 cup each dry white wine and fish stock or
   clam broth
1 cup heavy cream
1/4 teaspoon crumbled dried tarragon
salt and pepper to taste

Cut turbot into 1-inch pieces and purée in the blender. In a bowl beat together the egg whites and salt until foamy, add to the fish in the blender and purée until smooth. Place in the freezer 10 minutes to chill thoroughly. While the purée is chilling, skin salmon, remove any bones and cut in 6 serving-sized pieces. Place salmon in a buttered 9- by 12-inch baking dish and pour the wine and stock around the fish; set aside. Whip 3/4 cup of the cream until stiff and beat in the chilled fish mixture. Spread over the salmon. Bake in a 375° oven for 20 minutes or until top is golden brown and fish is cooked through.

Carefully pour juices from baking dish into a saucepan; keep fish warm. Cook pan juices over medium-high heat until reduced to 1/3 cup. Blend remaining 1/4 cup cream with the 2 egg yolks and pour in the hot broth, stirring to blend well. Return mixture to the saucepan and cook and stir until thickened. Season sauce with tarragon, salt and pepper. Pass the sauce to spoon over the fish.
Makes 6 servings

Quiches
Brioches

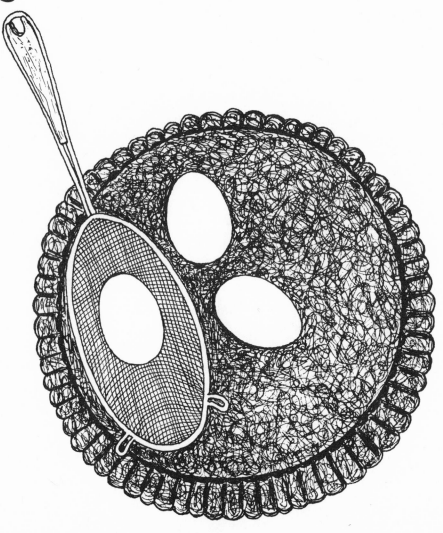

QUICHES

A quiche is an open-faced savory pastry filled with an egg custard to which various ingredients are added. The additions may be cheese, bacon, ham, mushrooms, salmon, crab or cooked vegetables such as asparagus tips, spinach or broccoli. A quiche may be baked in a flan ring placed on a baking sheet, a pie pan or fluted tart pan. A variety of pastries may be used. This custard pie is excellent hot, warm or at room temperature. It is appropriate as an appetizer, first-course dish or a luncheon or supper entrée.

WHOLE EGG PASTRY

1-1/4 cups all-purpose flour
1/2 teaspoon salt
1/4 pound butter
1 egg

Mix together flour and salt. Cut in butter until mixture is crumbly. Add egg and mix until the dough clings together in a ball. Pat into the bottom and sides of a 10-inch flan pan 2 inches deep with removable bottom.

VINEGAR-EGG PASTRY

This is an excellent, flaky savory pastry for quiches and vegetable pies.

1-1/4 cups all-purpose flour
1/4 pound butter or margarine
1/4 teaspoon salt
1 egg yolk
1 teaspoon cider vinegar
1 tablespoon cold water

Place flour, butter or margarine and salt in a mixing bowl and cut with a pastry blender until mixture is the consistency of oatmeal. Beat together until blended the egg yolk, vinegar and water and pour over the dry ingredients. Mix until blended and press into a ball. Chill 15 minutes. Roll out on a lightly floured board into a 13-inch round. Place pastry round in a 9-inch pie pan, press lightly against the sides and flute edges. Prick bottom about a dozen times with a fork. Chill to firm, about 15 minutes. Line pastry with foil and fill with dry beans. Prebake in a 400° oven for 8 minutes to set pastry. Remove beans and foil and bake 2 minutes longer. Remove from oven and allow to cool before filling.
Makes 1 9-inch pie shell

Quiches & Brioches

PRESS-IN EGG PASTRY

1-1/4 cups all-purpose flour
1/4 pound butter
1/2 teaspoon salt
2 egg yolks

Place in a mixing bowl the flour, butter and salt. Cut butter into flour until crumbly. Add egg yolks and mix until blended. Pat into a ball and press into bottom and sides of a 9-inch spring-form pan.

LEMON PASTRY

1-1/4 cups all-purpose flour
1/2 cup butter
1 teaspoon grated lemon peel
2 hard-cooked egg yolks
1 raw egg yolk
1/4 teaspoon salt

In a mixing bowl, combine flour and butter. Cut butter into flour until crumbly. Add remaining ingredients and mix just until blended. Pat dough into the bottom and sides of an 11-inch flan pan with 1-inch sides and removable bottom. Chill until firm. Prick bottom about a dozen times with a fork. Partially bake in a 400° oven 8 to 10 minutes.

QUICHE LORRAINE

This superb cheese pie is always meltingly good in its classic form, whether baked in a large round or in individual fluted shells as in France.

Vinegar-Egg Pastry, page 85
1-1/2 cups shredded Gruyère,
    Jarlsberg or Swiss cheese
4 eggs
1-3/4 cups half-and-half or milk
1/2 teaspoon salt
1/8 teaspoon ground nutmeg
8 strips bacon, crisply cooked and crumbled, or
3/4 cup diced cooked ham
2 teaspoons butter

First prepare pastry shell as directed in recipe. Sprinkle half the cheese over the shell. Beat eggs until blended and mix in half-and-half, salt and nutmeg. Stir in bacon and remaining cheese and spoon into the cheese-lined shell. Dot with butter. Bake in a 375° oven for 30 to 35 minutes or until custard is set, slightly puffed and golden brown.
Makes 6 servings

BEEF AND SAUSAGE QUICHE

This meat-filled pie is a hearty party quiche for a late supper or brunch. It is likely to become a family favorite as well.

Vinegar-Egg Pastry, page 85
1 large onion, finely chopped
1 tablespoon butter
2 mild Italian sausages (approximately 6 ounces)
1 pound lean ground beef
3 cloves garlic, minced
salt and pepper to taste
1 green onion, chopped
2 tablespoons finely chopped parsley
1 cup grated Gruyère or Swiss cheese
4 eggs
1-1/2 cups half-and-half or milk

First prepare pastry shell as directed in recipe. Using a large frying pan, sauté onion in butter until golden brown. Remove sausage meat from casings and add with beef to pan; cook until browned and crumbly. Remove from heat and mix in garlic, salt, pepper, green onion, parsley and half the cheese; set aside. Beat eggs until blended and stir in half-and-half and salt and pepper to taste. Spread meat mixture in the pastry-lined pan and pour egg mixture over. Sprinkle with remaining cheese. Bake in a 375° oven for 30 to 35 minutes or until set, slightly puffed and golden brown.
Makes 6 servings

MUSHROOM QUICHE

This vegetable pie makes a fine luncheon entrée or accompaniment to a roast for dinner.

Lemon Pastry, preceding
1/2 pound mushrooms, sliced (approximately 2 cups)
3 green onions (use only half of the green tops), chopped
4 tablespoons butter
4 eggs
1 cup milk
1/2 teaspoon each salt and crumbled dried tarragon
1 cup shredded Gruyère or Swiss cheese
3 tablespoons grated Parmesan cheese

Prepare pastry as directed in recipe and set aside. Sauté mushrooms and onions in 3 tablespoons of the butter just until glazed; remove from pan. Beat eggs until light and mix in milk, salt, tarragon, sautéed vegetables and shredded Gruyère. Pour into the pastry-lined pan. Dot with remaining 1 tablespoon of butter and sprinkle with Parmesan cheese. Bake in a 425° oven for 10 minutes; reduce heat to 350° and bake 30 minutes longer or until set. Let cool 10 minutes, remove pan sides and cut in wedges to serve.
Makes 10 servings

Quiches & Brioches

PARTY-SIZE QUICHE

A fluted flan pan with removable bottom works admirably to produce this oversized custard pie.

Whole Egg Pastry, page 85
8 eggs
2-1/2 cups milk
1 teaspoon salt
dash each pepper and ground nutmeg
1/4 cup shredded cooked ham or
    crisply cooked crumbled bacon
2 cups shredded Gruyère or Swiss cheese
1 tablespoon butter

Prepare pastry as directed in recipe and set aside. Beat eggs just until blended and mix in milk, salt, pepper, nutmeg and ham. Sprinkle cheese in the pastry-lined pan and pour in egg mixture. Dot top with shavings of butter. Bake in a 425° oven for 10 minutes; reduce heat to 375° and bake 30 minutes longer or until set and slightly puffed. Let cool a few minutes on a rack, then remove pan sides. Cut in wedges.
Makes 8 to 10 servings

Cheddar and Olive Party Quiche Substitute 1/2 cup sliced ripe olives and 2 cups grated Cheddar cheese for the ham and Gruyère cheese.

Crab and Shrimp Party Quiche For the ham, substitute 3/4 pound fresh cooked crab meat or shrimp, 3 chopped green onions and use 1-1/2 cups shredded Gruyère or Swiss cheese.

Mushroom and Jarlsberg Party Quiche For the ham and Gruyère, substitute 1/2 pound sliced mushrooms (approximately 2 cups), 2 shallots or green onions, chopped and sautéed in 2 tablespoons butter just until glazed, and 2 cups shredded Jarlsberg or Swiss cheese.

CRAB QUICHE

Delectable crab meat fills a quiche for a festive guest luncheon entrée.

Vinegar-Egg Pastry, page 85
1-1/4 cups shredded Gruyère or
  Jarlsberg cheese
6 ounces fresh crab meat or small cooked shrimp
2 shallots or green onions, finely chopped
1 tablespoon butter
2 tablespoons pale dry sherry
1/4 teaspoon crumbled dried tarragon
4 eggs
1-1/2 cups half-and-half or milk
salt and pepper to taste

First prepare pastry shell as directed in recipe. Sprinkle pastry shell with half the cheese. Sauté crab meat and shallots in butter for 1 minute. Add sherry and tarragon and cook down until liquid disappears; set aside. Beat eggs just until blended and stir in half-and-half, salt and pepper. Mix in crab meat mixture and remaining cheese. Spoon into cheese-lined shell. Bake in a 375° oven for 30 to 35 minutes or until custard is set, slightly puffed and golden brown.
Makes 6 servings

SALMON AND RIPE OLIVE QUICHE

A salmon pie is easily made from ingredients generally stocked in the pantry.

Vinegar-Egg Pastry, page 85
3/4 cup shredded Gruyère or Cheddar cheese
1 1-pound can salmon, drained
1/2 cup sliced ripe olives
1 shallot or green onion, chopped
2 tablespoons minced parsley
4 eggs
1-1/2 cups half-and-half or milk
1/2 teaspoon salt
1/2 teaspoon grated lemon peel
2 teaspoons butter

First prepare pastry shell as directed in recipe. Sprinkle half the cheese over the pastry shell. Separate salmon into bite-sized chunks and discard skin and bones. Place salmon chunks in the pastry shell and scatter olives, shallot, parsley and remaining cheese over. Beat eggs until blended and mix in half-and-half, salt and lemon peel. Pour the custard into the pastry shell and dot with butter. Bake in a 375° oven for 30 to 35 minutes or until custard is set, slightly puffed and golden brown.
Makes 6 servings

Quiches & Brioches

SPINACH TART

This festive vegetable pie makes a splendid side dish to roast beef or ham.

Lemon Pastry, page 86
1 large bunch spinach (approximately 1 pound), finely chopped
2 green onions, chopped
3 tablespoons butter
3 eggs
1/2 cup milk
1/2 teaspoon salt
dash each pepper and ground nutmeg
1 cup grated Gruyère or Swiss cheese
1/3 cup grated Parmesan cheese

Prepare pastry as directed in recipe and set aside. Sauté spinach and onions in 2 tablespoons of the butter just until spinach is barely wilted. Beat the eggs until blended and mix in milk, salt, pepper and nutmeg. Stir in vegetables and grated Gruyère. Turn egg mixture into the pastry-lined pan, dot with remaining 1 tablespoon butter and sprinkle with Parmesan cheese. Bake in a 425° oven for 10 minutes; reduce heat to 350° and bake 30 minutes longer or until set. Remove pan sides and cut in wedges to serve.
Makes 10 servings

SPINACH AND FETA PIE

The beloved Greek pairing of spinach and feta cheese is excellent in an open-face vegetable pie. Accompany with keftethes, the vinegar-glazed Greek meatballs.

Vinegar-Egg Pastry, page 85, or your favorite pastry
Dijon-style mustard
2 eggs
2 egg yolks
1/2 cup plain yogurt
1/2 cup milk
1 tablespoon chopped parsley
1/2 teaspoon each salt and crumbled dried tarragon
dash ground nutmeg
2 pounds spinach, chopped, cooked and drained
1/2 cup crumbled feta cheese
1 tablespoon butter, melted

First prepare pastry-lined pan and spread with a thin coating of mustard. Beat together eggs and egg yolks until blended and mix in yogurt, milk, parsley, salt, tarragon, nutmeg, spinach and feta. Spoon into the pastry-lined pan and drizzle top with melted butter. Bake in a 400° oven for 10 minutes; reduce heat to 350° and bake 25 minutes longer or until set. Let pie cool 5 minutes before cutting.
Makes 6 servings

TOMATO ROMANO PIE

This colorful tomato pie makes a bright accompaniment to a barbecue dinner.

Press-In Egg Pastry, page 86
3/4 cup grated Romano cheese
1 bunch green onions (approximately 6), chopped
2 to 3 firm, ripe tomatoes
flour, salt, pepper and crumbled dried basil
1/2 cup sliced ripe olives
2 eggs
1 cup heavy cream

Prepare Press-In Egg Pastry dough as directed in recipe. Roll out on a lightly floured board 3/16 inch thick and place in a 9-inch pie pan, fluting edges. Sprinkle pastry with 2 tablespoons of the cheese and half the onions and set aside.

Slice tomatoes about 1/2 inch thick and dip in flour to coat lightly. Sprinkle tomato slices with salt, pepper and basil to taste. Arrange tomato slices on pastry shell and sprinkle with remaining onions, half of the remaining cheese and olives. Beat eggs until blended and mix in cream. Pour egg mixture over tomatoes and sprinkle top with remaining cheese. Bake in a 400° oven for 35 minutes or until set and golden brown. Let cool slightly, cut in wedges and serve.
Makes 6 servings

ITALIAN SAUSAGE PIE

This outstanding entrée pie might star at a picnic or a special Italian supper. Round out the menu with *bagna cauda,* the hot anchovy and garlic butter for raw vegetables, and fresh melon or berries.

Press-In Egg Pastry, page 86
5 Italian garlic sausages (about 1 pound)
4 eggs
1 pound ricotta cheese
3/4 cup shredded Gruyère or Swiss cheese
3/4 cup grated Romano or Parmesan cheese
3 hard-cooked eggs, chopped
1/3 cup finely chopped parsley
2 green onions, chopped

Prepare pastry as directed in recipe and set aside. Simmer sausages in water to cover for 20 minutes; drain, cool slightly, remove skins and thinly slice. Beat eggs and ricotta together and mix in cheeses, sausage, hard-cooked eggs, parsley and onions. Spoon into the pastry-lined pan. Bake in a 375° oven for 30 minutes or until set. Serve warm or cold, cut in wedges.
Makes about 8 entrée servings, or
16 appetizer servings

Quiches & Brioches

ZWIEBELKUCHEN
(Onion Tart)

From southern Germany comes this savory onion and bacon pie, a delight for supper with coleslaw, pickled beets and garlic sausage.

1 package active dry yeast
3/4 cup lukewarm water (110° to 115°)
1/2 teaspoon salt
2 tablespoons safflower or corn oil
approximately 2 cups all-purpose flour
1/2 pound bacon, diced
2 pounds yellow onions, chopped
3 eggs
1 cup (1/2 pint) sour cream
2 tablespoons chopped parsley

Sprinkle yeast into warm water in a large mixing bowl and let stand until dissolved. Mix in 1/4 teaspoon of the salt, oil and flour, adding enough to make a soft dough. Turn out onto lightly floured board and knead until smooth and no longer sticky, about 5 minutes. Cover dough with a bowl or slip into a plastic bag and let rest 30 minutes. Butter a 10- by 15-inch jelly-roll pan or a 14-inch pizza pan and with oiled fingers press dough onto bottom and sides of pan.

Meanwhile, fry bacon until crisp, remove from pan and let drain on paper towels. Pour off all but 1/4 cup of the drippings. Sauté onions in drippings remaining in pan until golden. Let cool. Beat eggs until blended and mix in sour cream, the remaining 1/4 teaspoon of salt, cooked bacon, onions and parsley. Spread onion mixture over dough and let dough rise 15 minutes. Bake in a 425° oven for 25 minutes or until browned and set. Makes 8 to 10 servings

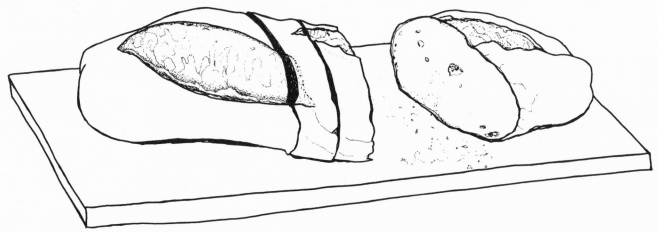

BRIOCHES

The buttery, egg-rich, yeast-leavened dough called brioche is not only delicious for coffee cakes and breads, but perfect for encasing foods which are baked *en croûte*. Poached Italian sausages, browned steak, fish and minced meat mixtures are all appropriate fillings for brioche dough.

When used for this purpose, the dough is often a batter-type mixture, so soft that it is not kneaded. Instead it is chilled after the first rising so it can be handled with ease as you roll it with a rolling pin. Extra dough scraps may be used to decorate the product by shaping free-form decorations of grapes and leaves, perhaps, or a braid or twisted coil. Small aspic cutters and cookie cutters are also useful for making cutouts of stars or daisies or whatever is appropriate as a decoration on top. The dough bakes into a golden brown crust, making a festive presentation for something as humble as a meatloaf. Brioche dough will keep refrigerated 2 to 3 days.

RICH BRIOCHE DOUGH

1 package active dry yeast
1/2 cup lukewarm water (110° to 115°)
1 tablespoon sugar
1/4 teaspoon salt
2-1/2 cups all-purpose flour
3 eggs
1/4 pound butter, at room temperature

Sprinkle yeast in warm water in a large mixing bowl; let stand until dissolved. Add the sugar, salt and 1/2 cup of the flour and beat well. Add the eggs, one at a time, and beat until smooth. Add the butter, a few tablespoons at a time, and beat until blended. Gradually add the remaining flour and beat hard for 5 minutes. (Do not knead the dough, as it is too soft.) Cover dough with a kitchen towel and let rise in a warm place 1 hour. Punch down and refrigerate at least 1 hour or overnight before using it.

EXTRA-RICH BRIOCHE DOUGH

3/4 cup butter, at room temperature
1 tablespoon sugar
3 eggs
1 teaspoon salt
1 package active dry yeast
1/4 cup lukewarm water (110° to 115°)
2 cups all-purpose flour

Beat butter and sugar until creamy and beat in eggs and salt. Sprinkle yeast into warm water, let stand until dissolved and mix into the egg mixture. Add 1 cup flour and beat well for 5 minutes. Gradually add remaining flour, beating well. Cover bowl with kitchen towel and let dough rise in a warm place until doubled in size, about 1 hour. Stir down and refrigerate at least 2 hours or as long as 2 days before using.

Quiches & Brioches

BEEF-STUFFED BRIOCHE

A muffin tin helps you shape these individual meat-filled brioches.

Extra-Rich Brioche Dough, page 93
3 medium-sized onions, chopped
1 tablespoon olive oil
3 pounds lean ground beef chuck
4 cloves garlic, minced
1/2 teaspoon each ground allspice and
   crumbled dried oregano
1/3 cup pine nuts
2 tablespoons red wine vinegar
2 eggs
3/4 cup sour cream or plain yogurt
1 green onion, minced
2 tablespoons chopped parsley

Prepare Extra-Rich Brioche Dough as directed. To make filling, sauté onions in oil until glazed. Add meat and cook until browned. Mix in garlic, allspice, oregano and nuts. Add vinegar and sauté 10 minutes; cool. Mix in eggs and set aside.

To assemble, divide dough into 12 equal parts and roll out each into a circle about 8 inches in diameter. Place about 1/2 cup of the meat filling in the center of a circle of dough and bring up the sides, sealing the edges and encasing the meat inside. Place brioche seam side down in a buttered muffin tin with the bulbous part extending above the rim. Repeat with remaining dough and filling. Let rise at room temperature 20 minutes. Bake in a 400° oven for 20 to 25 minutes or until golden brown. Serve hot, with a bowl of sour cream blended with green onion and parsley on the side. Makes 12 servings

STEAK IN BRIOCHE

Golden brioche dough provides a festive wrap for steak. Decorate the finished product with grapes, leaves, and a swirl of tendrils.

Rich Brioche Dough, page 93
1 2-pound piece top sirloin, about 1-1/2 inches thick
2 tablespoons butter
salt and pepper to taste
1/2 pound mushrooms, chopped
1/4 cup each finely chopped green onions
   and parsley
1 tablespoon brandy or sherry
1 egg yolk, beaten
1 tablespoon milk

Prepare Rich Brioche Dough as directed in recipe. Brown meat in 1 tablespoon of the butter, turning to brown both sides but not cooking through. Season with salt and pepper. Chill. Sauté mushrooms, onions and parsley in remaining butter until glazed. Add brandy and cook 1 minute; set aside. Roll out dough into a rectangle 3/16 inch thick. Place meat on center of dough. Spread mushroom

mixture on meat. Bring up lengthwise sides of dough and overlap on top. Fold in narrow ends, trimming off any excess dough. Place seam side down on a buttered baking sheet. Decorate top of pastry with cutouts made from any remaining scraps. Beat together egg yolk and milk and brush mixture onto brioche. Insert meat thermometer through crust into the center of the meat. Bake in a 425° oven for 25 to 30 minutes, or until thermometer registers 130° for rare meat. Remove from oven, place on a carving board and slice.
Makes 6 to 8 servings

FISH PIROGS

An egg-rich brioche dough encases salmon fillets for a handsome summer party entrée. The chilled dough is pliable, so it is easy to achieve an artistic design.

Rich Brioche Dough, page 93
2-1/2 pounds salmon, turbot or sole fillets
fish stock as needed
1 tablespoon freshly squeezed lemon juice
1 bunch green onions (approximately 6), chopped
3 tablespoons butter
1/2 pound mushrooms, sliced
   (approximately 2 cups)
1/4 cup chopped parsley
6 hard-cooked eggs, chopped
1 egg white, lightly beaten
sour cream
caviar

Prepare Rich Brioche Dough as directed in recipe. Poach fish fillets in stock just until tender, about 5 to 10 minutes depending upon thickness of fillets. Remove from pan and let cool; peel skin off salmon fillets. Sprinkle fillets with lemon juice and set aside. Sauté onions in butter until glazed. Add mushrooms and sauté just until glazed. Mix in parsley and set aside.

For free-form fish pastries, first divide brioche dough in half. Roll out each half into 2 3/16-inch-thick triangles, each about 14 inches long, 5 inches wide at midpoint and 9 inches at the base. Place 1 triangle of dough on a buttered baking sheet. Layer with half each of the sautéed vegetables, chopped eggs, poached fish and cover with second triangle of dough, pinching edges to seal. Repeat procedure to make a second fish from the remaining ingredients. With a small, thin-bladed knife, score wide end of each pastry to make tail design. Slash sides at midpoint for fins and slash at narrow end for mouth and eye. With scissors, snip top crust in 2 or 3 rows to make scales. Brush entire surface of pastries with beaten egg white. Bake in a 375° oven for 30 to 35 minutes, or until nicely browned. Place on a board and serve warm or cold with sour cream and caviar.
Makes 10 servings

Quiches & Brioches

MEAT PIROG

This festive meat pie is ready-made for guests or an outing. You can make it in advance and serve it cold or reheat it. It freezes well in case you wish to stash one away for another occasion.

Extra-Rich Brioche Dough, page 93
2 large onions, finely chopped
1 tablespoon butter
2 pounds lean ground beef
1 pound raw ground turkey or veal
3 cloves garlic, minced
2-1/2 teaspoons salt
1 teaspoon dry mustard
1 tablespoon each Worcestershire sauce and
   red wine vinegar
1/2 teaspoon each ground allspice and
   crumbled dried oregano
1/4 cup pale dry sherry
1 cup shredded Gruyère or Jarlsberg cheese
3 eggs, lightly beaten
1 egg white, lightly beaten

Prepare Extra-Rich Brioche Dough as directed in recipe. Using a large frying pan, sauté onions in butter until glazed; add meats and garlic and cook until browned. Drain off any extra fat. Add salt, mustard, Worcestershire, vinegar, allspice, oregano and sherry and simmer, uncovered, for 5 minutes to reduce juices. If necessary, remove meat to a bowl with a slotted spoon, boil down the juices until reduced to a glaze and add to meat. Let cool slightly, then mix in cheese and whole eggs. Divide brioche dough in half and roll out each piece into a circle about 16 inches in diameter and 1/8 inch thick. Place half of the meat on half of one of the pastry circles, leaving a 1-inch border, and fold over pastry, making a half-moon shape. Pinch edges to seal. Place on a greased baking sheet and repeat with remaining pastry and filling. Brush top of pastry with lightly beaten egg white. Bake in a 425° oven for 20 minutes or until browned. Transfer to a board to serve. If desired, accompany with Shallot Sauce (page 108).
Makes 12 servings

CREPES
PASTA

Crepes & Pasta

CRÊPES

The French word for pancake is crêpe, a thin and light egg-rich one. They may be rolled, folded or stacked and filled or sauced with a wide variety of savory and sweet ingredients—minced meats, cooked vegetables, seafood, fruit, ice cream or liqueurs.

There are many choices in crêpe pans. The best crêpe pan is heavier than an omelet pan, thereby better retaining the heat. Pans are available in iron, stainless steel, copper and stainless, and heavy-weight aluminum. Some are teflon-lined; the T-fal brand is a good one. A relatively new process of cooking crêpes on the underneath side of the pan is available with crêpe makers or griddles. These produce a beautiful, fragile thin crêpe that is cooked on one side only. Crêpe pans demand the same care with seasoning and wiping with paper towels, rather than washing, that omelet pans need.

Crêpe batter should be the consistency of heavy cream. It is wise to allow the crêpe batter to sit for at least 30 minutes so the flour particles expand in the liquid. This insures a tender, light, thin crêpe. Use just enough batter to coat the crêpe pan thinly—a slightly lacy crêpe is more desirable than a thick one. Crêpes may be cooked on one side only.

Crêpes may be made in advance, stacked, covered and refrigerated for 2 or 3 days before using. They may also be packaged airtight and frozen. Thaw before using.

Spinach Crêpes Mix chopped, lightly cooked spinach with béchamel or Mornay Sauce (page 62), and roll up inside crêpes. Bake in a 375° oven for 10 to 15 minutes or until heated through and serve with sour cream seasoned with minced chives or shallots and salt and pepper.

Mushroom Crêpes Bind sautéed sliced mushrooms with Mornay Sauce (page 62). Sprinkle filling with grated Gruyère cheese, and roll up inside crêpes. Bake in a 375° oven for 10 to 15 minutes or until heated through.

Lox and Cheese Crêpes Make a spread of cream cheese, sour cream, chopped smoked salmon, minced chives and grated lemon peel. Roll up inside crêpes. Serve at room temperature or chilled.

Joe's Special Crêpes Fill crêpes with the ground beef and spinach mixture called Joe's Special (page 113), roll up and bake in a 375° oven for 10 to 15 minutes or until heated through.

Egg and Caviar Crêpes Fill small crêpes with a chopped hard-cooked egg and chive spread, roll up, and top with sour cream and caviar. Serve cold.

SAVORY CRÊPES

1 cup milk
3 eggs
3/4 cup all-purpose flour
1/4 teaspoon salt
butter as needed

Place in a blender container or beat together in a mixing bowl with a wire whisk, the milk, eggs, flour and salt, blending until smooth. Let batter stand at least 30 minutes. Heat a 6-inch crêpe pan over medium heat, add 1/2 teaspoon butter, and tilt pan to coat surface. Pour in just enough batter to coat pan (about 2 tablespoons) and tilt pan to cover entire surface. Cook until golden brown on the edges and dry on top, less than 1 minute. Turn out onto a plate. Repeat with remaining batter, adding butter as needed. Stack and use immediately or let cool and refrigerate.
Makes 16 crepes

HAM AND SWISS CHEESE CRÊPES

16 Savory Crêpes, preceding
2 cups ground cooked ham
1 egg
1 shallot or green onion, chopped
1 teaspoon Dijon-style mustard
1 cup (1/2 pint) sour cream
1-1/4 cups shredded Swiss or Samsoe cheese
2 tablespoons butter, melted

Prepare crêpes as directed in recipe and set aside. Mix together the ham, egg, chopped shallot, mustard, 3 tablespoons of the sour cream and the cheese. Spoon about 1/3 cup of the filling onto each crêpe and roll up into a cylinder. Place seam side down in a buttered baking dish. Repeat with remaining filling and crêpes. Drizzle melted butter over crêpes and bake in a 375° oven for 10 to 15 minutes or until heated through. Spoon a dollop of sour cream on each serving.
Makes 8 servings

CREPES & PASTA

CHICKEN OR SEAFOOD CRÊPES

This versatile luncheon entrée is easily made in advance.

16 Savory Crêpes, page 99
3 tablespoons each butter and flour
1-1/4 cups half-and-half, milk or part chicken
   or fish stock
2 egg yolks
1/4 cup heavy cream
salt, pepper and ground nutmeg to taste
1/2 cup grated Parmesan cheese
3 cups diced cooked chicken meat or
   cooked shrimp, crab or lobster meat

Prepare Savory Crêpes as directed in recipe and set aside. Melt butter in a saucepan and blend in flour. Cook and stir over low heat for 2 minutes. Heat liquid and gradually pour into the butter-flour paste. Stirring, cook until thickened. Beat egg yolks with heavy cream. Blend some of the hot sauce into the yolk mixture and then add yolk mixture to saucepan, blending thoroughly. Mix in seasonings, half the cheese and chicken or seafood. Spoon about 1/3 cup of the filling in a ribbon on the lower third of each crêpe and roll into a cylinder. Place seam side down in a buttered baking dish. Repeat with remaining filling and crêpes. Sprinkle tops with remaining cheese. Bake in a 375° oven for 10 to 15 minutes or until heated through.
Makes 8 servings

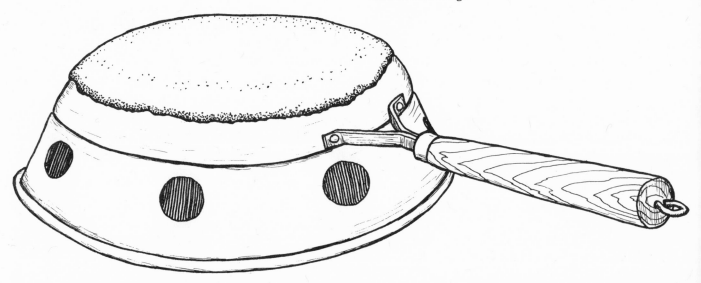

SILVER BLINTZES

Cornstarch creates a particularly tender crêpe for these Jewish blintzes.

Cornstarch Crêpes, following
1/2 pound farmers' cheese
4 ounces cream cheese
1 egg yolk
2 tablespoons sugar
1/2 teaspoon vanilla extract
butter
sour cream and cherry preserves

Prepare Cornstarch Crêpes as directed in recipe. Beat cheeses together and mix in egg yolk, sugar and vanilla. Place a tablespoon of filling on the center of the unbrowned side of each pancake and fold in sides to make an envelope shape. Place seam side down in a large buttered baking dish. Dot with butter and bake in a 375° oven for 20 minutes, or until heated through. Serve with a spoonful of sour cream and preserves on each.
Makes 16 blintzes

CORNSTARCH CRÊPES

3 eggs
1 cup plus 2 tablespoons milk
3/4 cup cornstarch
2 tablespoons butter, melted
1/8 teaspoon each salt and baking soda
butter as needed

Place in a blender container or beat together in a mixing bowl with a wire whisk, the eggs, milk, cornstarch, melted butter, salt and baking soda, blending until smooth. Let stand at least 30 minutes. Heat a lightly buttered 6-inch crêpe pan, spoon in 2 tablespoons of the batter and cook crêpe on 1 side only until lightly browned. Repeat with remaining batter, adding butter to the pan as needed and stacking crêpes as they are cooked.
Makes 16 crêpes

CREPES & PASTA

FRESH EGG PASTA

A pasta machine speeds the process of making homemade noodles. Without this aid they are a tedious chore, but the results are rewarding.

3 cups all-purpose flour
1 teaspoon salt
1/4 cup water
3 tablespoons safflower or olive oil
3 eggs

Place flour and salt in a mixing bowl and make a well in the center. Add water, oil and eggs. With your finger tips or a fork, mix until flour is blended in and shape into a ball. Knead on a lightly floured board until dough is smooth and elastic, about 10 minutes. Cover with plastic wrap and let rest for 10 minutes before rolling out.

For Cannelloni Noodles Divide dough into 8 equal portions. On a lightly floured board, roll each portion into a 10-inch square, 1/16 inch thick. Cut into 4 pieces, each 5 inches square. Cover until all dough is rolled and cut. (Or use a pasta machine to roll out dough into a 5-inch width and cut into 5-inch squares.)

To cook, in a large, shallow pan, bring a 1/2 inch salted water, flavored with 1 tablespoon olive oil, to a boil. Place 4 or 5 noodles in water and cook for 2 minutes or until just tender. With a spatula lift from water and let drain on a towel. Repeat until all noodles are cooked. Makes 32 cannelloni noodles.

For Fettuccine or Tagliarini Noodles Divide dough into 4 portions. Feed through a pasta machine or on a lightly floured board roll out 1/16 inch thick and cut by hand to desired width or approximately 1/4 inch wide for fettuccine and 1/8 inch wide for tagliarini.

To cook, drop noodles into at least 4 quarts rapidly boiling salted water flavored with 1 tablespoon olive oil. Return to boil and cook for 2 minutes or until tender. Drain. Makes about 1 pound fettuccine or tagliarini noodles.

CARBONARA

Egg yolks are blended with melted cheese to make a creamy sauce for this pasta dish. Serve with grilled Italian sausages for a complete entrée.

6 strips bacon, cut in 1-inch pieces
1 large onion, finely chopped
1 pound fresh Tagliarini Noodles, preceding, or
   purchased
4 tablespoons butter, melted
3 egg yolks, lightly beaten
1/2 cup chopped parsley
2 ounces prosciutto or cooked ham,
   cut in julienne
1 cup diced Gruyère or Samsoe cheese
1-1/2 cups freshly grated Parmesan cheese
freshly ground pepper

Sauté bacon until crisp; remove bacon from pan and let drain on paper towels. Sauté onion in bacon drippings; transfer to a bowl and set aside. Cook Tagliarini as directed in boiling salted water until tender, about 2 to 3 minutes. Drain, rinse under cold water and transfer to a bowl or large platter. Spoon over the Tagliarini the butter, egg yolks, sautéed onion, bacon, parsley, prosciutto, diced cheese and half the Parmesan and mix until noodles are coated. Grind over the pepper. Pass remaining Parmesan at the table.
Makes 6 servings

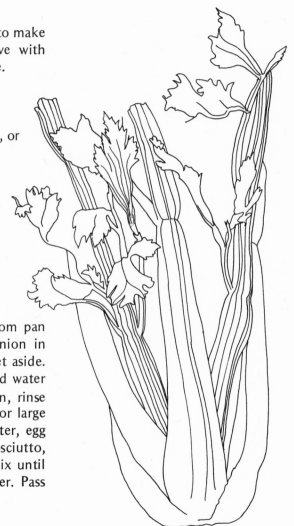

CREPES & PASTA

FLORENTINE CANNELLONI

Lovely fresh pasta makes a flavorful wrapper for a savory veal and ricotta stuffing. Cannelloni freezes well so it's wise to assemble a large batch once you get involved in the production.

Tomato Béchamel Sauce, following
2 large onions, chopped
4 tablespoons butter
3 cloves garlic, minced
2 pounds ground veal
2 cups (1 pint) ricotta cheese
1 cup grated Parmesan cheese
5 egg yolks
1-1/2 teaspoons salt
1/2 teaspoon crumbled dried tarragon
1/4 teaspoon ground nutmeg
1 bunch spinach (approximately 1 pound),
  chopped and cooked until wilted, or
1 10-ounce package frozen chopped spinach,
  thawed and drained
1 pound fresh Cannelloni Noodles, page 102,
  or purchased (green, if desired)
2 pounds Teleme or Monterey Jack cheese,
  thinly sliced

Prepare Tomato Béchamel Sauce as directed below and set aside. Sauté onions in butter until golden. Add garlic and veal and cook just until meat is browned. Mix together the ricotta, Parmesan, egg yolks, salt, tarragon, nutmeg and spinach and stir into the browned meat; set aside. Cut Cannelloni Noodles into desired lengths, about 4 to 5 inches long, and cook in boiling salted water until al dente; drain on paper toweling, placing them flat. Pour a thin layer of Tomato Béchamel Sauce in 2 large ovenproof shallow baking dishes. To assemble cannelloni, place about 3 tablespoons of the spinach-veal filling in a ribbon down the center of each piece of pasta and roll up to enclose. Place seam side down in baking dish. Repeat with remaining noodles and filling. Cover cannelloni with remaining sauce and arrange cheese on top. If desired, you may freeze 1 dish at this point; thaw before baking. Bake cannelloni in a 425° oven for 10 to 12 minutes, or until heated through.
Makes about 4 dozen cannelloni,
or 16 to 20 servings

Tomato Béchamel Sauce For the tomato sauce, sauté 1 medium-sized onion, chopped, in 2 tablespoons butter until glazed. Add 6 to 8 ripe tomatoes, peeled and chopped, or 1 28-ounce can puréed tomatoes, 1 teaspoon each salt and sugar, and 2 tablespoons minced fresh basil or 1-1/2 teaspoons crumbled dried basil. Simmer uncovered until reduced by half.

For the béchamel sauce, melt 2/3 cup butter and stir in 1/2 cup all-purpose flour. Cook, stirring constantly, 2 minutes. Gradually stir in 2 cups heated milk and 1 cup hot rich chicken stock and cook, stirring constantly, until thickened. Remove from heat and combine béchamel sauce with tomato sauce.

STUFFED MEAT ROLL WITH TOMATO SAUCE

Eggs and parsley form a spiral with steak in this southern Italian dish. It is excellent with pasta.

1 2-pound piece boneless round steak, cut
    1/2 inch thick
2 hard-cooked eggs, chopped
1/4 cup finely chopped parsley
1/4 cup freshly shredded Parmesan or
    Romano cheese
1 teaspoon crumbled dried basil, or
3 teaspoons chopped fresh basil
4 cloves garlic, minced
salt and pepper to taste
1 tablespoon olive oil
1 large onion, chopped
6 to 8 medium-sized ripe tomatoes, peeled
    and chopped, or
1 28-ounce can puréed tomatoes (preferably
    Italian plum style)
1 cup dry red wine
1/2 teaspoon crumbled dried oregano
1 pound fresh Tagliarini Noodles, page 102,
    or purchased

Trim fat from meat, lay meat between 2 sheets of waxed paper and pound lightly until slightly thinner and of even thickness. Mix together the eggs, parsley, cheese, half of the basil and 2 cloves of the garlic and spread over the meat. Sprinkle with salt and pepper to taste. Roll up and tie with string at 1-1/2-inch intervals. Using a large frying pan or Dutch oven, brown meat in oil, turning to brown all sides. Add onion and sauté until glazed. Add tomatoes, wine, oregano and remaining garlic and basil. Season sauce lightly with salt and pepper and cover and simmer 45 minutes to 1 hour or until meat is tender. Just before meat is cooked, cook Tagliarini in boiling salted water until al dente; drain and place on a large platter. To serve, spoon the hot tomato sauce over Tagliarini, cut meat roll into 3/4-inch-thick slices and place on top.
Makes about 8 servings

Eggy Entrees & Sauces

ROLLED EGG PANCAKE WITH PORK
(Tan-Chuan)

This Oriental entrée is particularly eye-catching with pinwheels of egg pancake encircling a savory pork filling.

5 eggs
peanut oil as needed
1/2 pound ground pork shoulder
2 teaspoons each soy sauce and cornstarch
1 tablespoon pale dry sherry
1/4 teaspoon salt
3 tablespoons finely chopped water chestnuts
1 green onion, chopped
1-1/2 pounds green peas, shelled, or
1 10-ounce package frozen petite peas

For the pancakes, beat 4 of the eggs with 2 teaspoons peanut oil until blended. Lightly oil an 8-inch frying pan and heat over medium-high heat. Pour in one-third of the egg batter and tilt pan to coat bottom. Cook until set, lift out and repeat, making 2 more egg pancakes and adding oil to pan as needed. Set aside. Mix together the pork, soy sauce, cornstarch, sherry, salt, water chestnuts, onion and the remaining egg, lightly beaten. Spread one-third of filling over surface of each pancake and roll up like a jelly roll. Place on a rack and steam over 1/2 inch of gently boiling water for 20 minutes. Meanwhile cook peas in boiling salted water until tender, about 3 to 5 minutes; drain and turn out on a platter. Slice pancake rolls diagonally in 1-inch pieces and arrange over the peas.
Makes 4 luncheon servings, or 8 servings as one of several entrées of an Oriental dinner

JAPANESE STEAMED EGG CUSTARD
(Chawan Mushi)

This custard is traditionally cooked on a bamboo Chinese steamer in a wok, but a roasting pan or a Dutch oven, fitted with a rack placed over water level, works just as well.

6 eggs
1/2 teaspoon salt
1-1/2 tablespoons dry sherry
2 cups hot water
2/3 cup ground pork or finely chopped
    fresh raw shrimp
12 watercress sprigs

Beat eggs until foamy and mix in salt and sherry. Gradually beat in water and stir in pork or shrimp and watercress. Pour into 6 buttered 6-ounce custard cups. Place on a rack over simmering water, cover and steam 25 to 30 minutes or until set.
Makes 6 servings

Eggy Entrees & Sauces

FILA MEAT ROLL

In this economical version of beef Wellington, fila makes a crispy wrapper around a sausage-stuffed meatloaf. The combination of meats may be a surprise but the result is a savory one.

3 mild Italian sausages (approximately 1/2 pound)
2 medium-sized onions, finely chopped
2 tablespoons butter
3 eggs
3/4 cup milk
3 slices white or whole-wheat bread, broken up
2-1/2 teaspoons salt
freshly ground pepper to taste
3 cloves garlic, chopped
2 teaspoons Worcestershire sauce
3 tablespoons chopped parsley
2 pounds lean ground beef
1 pound ground raw turkey meat
8 sheets (approximately 1/4 pound) fila dough
melted butter as needed
Shallot Sauce, following

Place sausages in a saucepan, cover with water and simmer 15 minutes; set aside. Sauté onion in butter until golden; set aside. In a blender container place eggs, milk, bread, salt, pepper, garlic, Worcestershire and parsley and blend until smooth. Empty blender container into a bowl, add the sautéed onion and ground meats and mix thoroughly until blended. Pat into a 4- by 14-inch log on a lightly greased baking pan. Make a crevice down the center of the log and place sausages, end to end, into depression. Bring meat up and around to encase the sausages in the center. Bake in a 375° oven for 40 minutes; let cool before wrapping in fila.

Lay out fila and cover with clear plastic wrap. Brush one sheet lightly with melted butter and arrange remaining sheets of fila on top, buttering each one and overlapping to make a rectangle about 18 by 20 inches. Place meat roll across a narrow side and roll up. Tuck in ends. Place on a buttered baking sheet and brush with melted butter. Bake in a 400° oven for 30 minutes or until fila is crispy and brown. While meat is baking, prepare Shallot Sauce. Remove meat roll from oven, transfer to a platter or board and cut into 1-inch slices. Serve with Shallot Sauce.
Makes 12 servings

Shallot Sauce Mix together 1/2 cup each sour cream and plain yogurt, 2 tablespoons chopped parsley, 1 shallot or green onion, chopped, and dash freshly ground pepper.

BASTILLA

The fascinating Moroccan chicken pie is fun to present in individual servings, each wrapped in crispy fila layers. (Traditionally it is made in one huge pie, but then it is messy to cut and serve.)

1 large onion, finely chopped
2/3 cup butter
1 tablespoon finely shredded ginger root, or
1-1/2 teaspoons ground ginger
1-1/2 teaspoons ground cinnamon
1 teaspoon ground cumin
1/2 teaspoon each ground turmeric and allspice
dash cayenne pepper
4 chicken thighs
4 chicken breasts
1 teaspoon salt
1/4 cup chopped fresh coriander
1 clove garlic, minced
6 eggs
3/4 cup slivered blanched almonds
1 tablespoon granulated sugar
6 to 8 sheets fila dough
1-1/2 tablespoons powdered sugar
whole blanched almonds

Sauté onion in 2 tablespoons of the butter until glazed. Add ginger root, 1/2 teaspoon of the cinnamon, cumin, turmeric, allspice and cayenne and sauté a few minutes. Add chicken parts and brown on all sides. Season with salt and add coriander, garlic and 1 cup water. Cover and simmer breasts 20 minutes and remove from pan. Continue cooking thighs, covered, for 10 to 15 minutes, or until cooked through. Remove chicken from pan and let cool. Remove skin and bones from chicken parts and cut meat into 1/2-inch strips; set aside. Bring broth in pan to a boil and reduce to 1 cup; let cool slightly.

Beat eggs and blend in the 1 cup broth. Melt 1 tablespoon of the butter in a large frying pan. Pour in egg mixture and cook, lifting with a spatula to allow uncooked portion to flow underneath, until eggs are just set. Remove from pan and set aside.

Melt 1 tablespoon of the butter in a small frying pan and sauté slivered almonds until golden. Turn out of pan and mix with the granulated sugar and 1/2 teaspoon of the cinnamon. Melt remaining butter. Lay out fila sheets and cover with plastic wrap. Place 1 sheet of fila on a board and brush with melted butter. Fold the sheet in to make a 9-inch square. Spoon a small mound of the cooked egg mixture, the chicken and the toasted almonds in the center and fold the edges of the square over the top of the filling to make a package. Place seam side down on a buttered baking sheet.

Repeat with remaining fila and filling. Brush tops with melted butter. Bake in a 350° oven for 20 to 25 minutes, or until golden brown. Remove from baking sheet. Mix together powdered sugar and remaining 1/2 teaspoon of cinnamon and sift over the top. With a knife, score through the sugar making a diamond pattern and place a whole almond in center. Cool slightly before serving.
Makes 6 to 8 servings

Eggy Entrees & Sauces

SPANAKOPITA
(Spinach Pie)

The delectable Greek spinach pie with its marvelous crispy layers of fila pastry is a perfect vegetarian entrée or a choice companion to roast beef or lamb for dinner. It may be made well in advance as it is good hot, warm or cold.

2 bunches spinach (approximately 2 pounds)
1 bunch Swiss chard or chicory (approximately 1-1/2 pounds)
1 bunch green onions (approximately 6)
1 bunch parsley (approximately 4 ounces)
6 eggs, lightly beaten
1/4 cup olive oil
2 teaspoons salt
freshly ground pepper to taste
1/2 teaspoon crumbled dried oregano
1/3 pound feta cheese, crumbled
3/4 cup shredded Monterey Jack cheese
1 cup grated Parmesan cheese
12 sheets fila dough
approximately 6 tablespoons butter, melted

Finely chop the spinach, chard, onions and parsley. Place in a large towel and squeeze to dry thoroughly. Mix beaten eggs with the oil, salt, pepper and oregano. Mix cheeses with greens in a large bowl, pour the beaten eggs over and mix to blend. Lay out fila and cover with clear plastic wrap to keep from drying out. Line a buttered 9- by 13-inch baking dish with 1 sheet of fila, brush with melted butter and cover with 5 more sheets of fila, brushing each with melted butter and letting fila extend over sides of dish. Place greens in the fila-lined dish and smooth top. Fold any overlapping fila back over the greens. Arrange 6 or more sheets of fila on top, brushing each with melted butter and cut or fold them to fit top of pan. Brush top with melted butter. Use a sharp knife to cut through top layers of fila, making 3 lengthwise cuts and 5 crosswise cuts to make squares. Bake in a 375° oven for 50 minutes, or until greens are tender and pastry is golden. Remove from baking dish and let cool on a rack. Finish cutting through into squares to serve. Makes 24 pieces, or about 12 servings

MUSHROOM AND EGG RAMEKINS

Small stoneware pots, French pâté molds, and individual soufflé dishes make charming containers for this luncheon entrée. Consider it also as a first-course dish. It is one you may assemble ahead and bake just before serving.

3 slices firm white bread, cut in 1/2-inch cubes
6 tablespoons butter
3/4 pound mushrooms, sliced
   (approximately 3 cups)
salt and pepper to taste
1 clove garlic, minced
1/2 teaspoon crumbled dried tarragon
1 tablespoon pale dry sherry
3/4 cup sour cream
3 hard-cooked eggs, chopped
1/2 cup grated Gruyère or Swiss cheese

Using a large frying pan, sauté bread in 3 tablespoons of the butter until golden. Distribute croûtons in the bottom of 6 buttered baking dishes with about 3/4-cup capacity. Sauté mushrooms in remaining butter just until glazed. Season with salt, pepper, garlic and tarragon. Add sherry and cook down until juices are reduced slightly. Remove from heat and stir in sour cream and eggs. Spoon into the baking dishes and sprinkle each with cheese. Bake in a 425° oven 8 to 10 minutes or until cheese melts.
Makes 6 servings

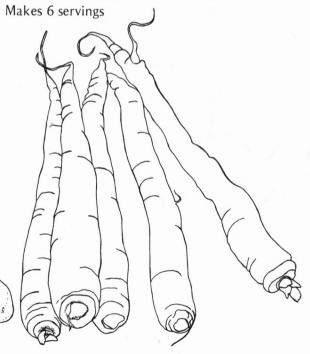

Eggy Entrees & Sauces

MOUSSAKA

Moussaka is excellent layered with zucchini instead of the typical eggplant. This is a good dish for a large buffet party accompanied by lemon-basted baked chicken, country salad, Cheese Pitas and Ravani.

Meat Sauce, following
2 pounds medium-sized zucchini
1/3 cup olive oil
6 tablespoons each butter and flour
3 cups milk, heated
1/2 teaspoon salt
1/8 teaspoon each ground nutmeg and pepper
4 eggs
1/3 cup fine dry bread crumbs
1 cup freshly grated Romano or Parmesan cheese

Prepare Meat Sauce as directed and set aside. Trim ends from zucchini and slice lengthwise on the diagonal about 1/3 inch thick. Sauté zucchini in oil, turning, until crisp-tender. In a saucepan, melt butter, blend in flour and cook and stir 2 minutes. Gradually stir in milk and, stirring constantly, cook until thickened. Season with salt, nutmeg and pepper. Beat eggs until blended, stir in some of the hot sauce, return to saucepan and stir until well blended; set aside. Arrange half the zucchini in a buttered 9- by 13-inch baking pan about 2-1/2 inches deep. Mix Meat Sauce with crumbs and half the cheese and spread half of it over the zucchini. Cover with another layer of zucchini and Meat Sauce. Spoon custard sauce over the top and sprinkle with remaining cheese. Bake in a 350° oven for 50 minutes or until set and golden brown. Let stand 10 to 15 minutes, then cut into squares. Makes about 12 servings

Meat Sauce Using a large frying pan, sauté 2 medium-sized onions, chopped, in 2 tablespoons butter until golden. Add 2 pounds lean ground beef or lamb and cook until meat is browned. Add 2 cloves garlic, minced, 1 8-ounce can tomato sauce, 3 tablespoons minced parsley, 1/4 cup red wine vinegar, 1-1/2 teaspoons salt and 1/4 teaspoon each ground cinnamon and allspice. Cover and simmer 30 to 40 minutes.

CHILES RELLENOS CASSEROLE

This makes a fine side dish to roast turkey or ham. Or present it for brunch along with assorted grilled sausages.

2 bunches green onions (approximately 12),
   thinly sliced
2 tablespoons butter
1 14-ounce can chopped green chiles
1 clove garlic, minced
8 eggs
3/4 cup half-and-half or milk
1/2 teaspoon salt
1/8 teaspoon each crumbled dried oregano,
   ground cumin and pepper
1-1/4 cups each shredded Monterey Jack and
   Cheddar cheese

Sauté onions in butter until glazed; remove from heat and stir in chiles and garlic. Beat eggs until blended and mix in half-and-half, salt and seasonings, sautéed vegetables and 1 cup each of the Monterey Jack and Cheddar cheese. Pour into a buttered 2-quart baking dish. Bake in a 350° oven for 30 minutes. Sprinkle with remaining 1/2 cup cheese and bake 5 to 10 minutes longer, or until set and lightly browned.
Makes 8 servings

JOE'S SPECIAL SANDWICHES

This San Francisco specialty is traditionally served as an entrée, *sans* bread. It makes a great sandwich as well, mounded on garlic-buttered toasted sourdough bread.

2 shallots or green onions, chopped
1/4 pound mushrooms, thinly sliced
   (approximately 1 cup)
1 tablespoon butter
1 pound ground beef chuck
1 clove garlic, minced
1/2 teaspoon salt
freshly ground pepper to taste
3/4 pound spinach, finely chopped
3 eggs
1/2 cup shredded Parmesan cheese
4 slices sourdough French bread, spread with
   garlic butter and toasted

Sauté shallots and mushrooms in butter until glazed. Add beef and brown lightly. Season with garlic, salt and pepper. Add spinach and cook just until wilted, about 2 minutes. Break in eggs and add cheese; cook and stir until set. Serve over hot sourdough bread.
Makes 4 servings

Eggy Entrees & Sauces

VEAL AND ARTICHOKES WITH LEMON SAUCE

Tangy lemon sauce binds this Mediterranean meat and vegetable stew.

2 pounds boneless veal, cut in 1-inch cubes
2 tablespoons butter
1 medium-sized onion, chopped
2 cloves garlic, minced
salt and pepper to taste
1/2 teaspoon crumbled dried tarragon
1-1/2 cups beef stock
2 8-ounce packages frozen artichoke hearts
2 eggs
1 tablespoon cornstarch
3 tablespoons freshly squeezed lemon juice
chopped parsley

Using a large frying pan, brown meat in butter on all sides. Add onion and cook until golden. Add garlic, salt, pepper and tarragon. Pour in stock. Cover and simmer 1-1/2 hours or until meat is tender. Add artichoke hearts and cook through, about 7 minutes. Beat eggs and blend in cornstarch and lemon juice. Gradually whisk in some of the hot broth. Return to the pan and cook and stir just until thickened. Sprinkle with parsley just before serving.
Makes 4 to 6 servings

MEATBALLS WITH LEMON SAUCE

Greek egg-lemon sauce and rice-flecked meatballs are a refreshing combination.

1 pound lean ground beef
1/2 pound lean ground veal
2 tablespoons each chopped onion and parsley
2 cloves garlic, minced
1-1/2 teaspoons salt
1/2 teaspoon crumbled dried oregano
freshly ground pepper
1/4 cup long-grain rice
2 cups rich beef stock
flour
2 eggs
1 tablespoon cornstarch
3 tablespoons freshly squeezed lemon juice

Mix together the beef, veal, onion, parsley, garlic, salt, oregano, pepper and rice and 1/4 cup of the beef stock. Shape mixture into 1-1/4-inch balls and roll in flour. Heat remaining broth to boiling, add meatballs, cover and simmer 35 minutes or until rice is tender. Beat eggs until blended, then beat in cornstarch and lemon juice. Pour some of the broth from the meat into the egg-lemon mixture, return to the pan and cook and stir until thickened. Serve accompanied with hot pita bread, if desired.
Makes 6 servings

TARRAGON POACHED CHICKEN

A creamy wine sauce served with a succulent bird produces a festive company entrée.

1 medium-sized onion, chopped
1 carrot, chopped
2 tablespoons butter
1 3-pound fryer chicken
salt and pepper to taste
1 cup dry vermouth or dry white wine
1/2 cup chicken stock
1 clove garlic, minced
1 teaspoon crumbled dried tarragon
2 egg yolks
1/4 cup heavy cream

Sauté onion and carrot in 1 tablespoon of the butter in a large Dutch oven. Push vegetables to the sides of the pan. Wash chicken, pat dry, season with salt and pepper and sauté whole in remaining butter, turning to brown all sides. Add vermouth, chicken stock, garlic and tarragon. Cover and simmer 1 hour, or until chicken is tender. Transfer chicken to a platter and keep warm. Strain pan juices into a saucepan, discarding vegetables, and boil down until reduced to about 3/4 cup. Beat egg yolks with cream and pour part of the reduced sauce into the cream mixture. Return to the saucepan and cook, stirring, until thickened. Pour into a sauce bowl. Carve chicken and pass sauce to spoon over at the table.
Makes 4 to 6 servings

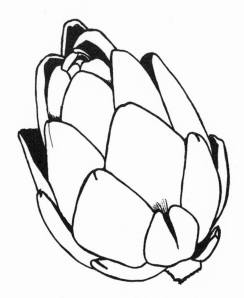

Eggy Entrees & Sauces

TURBOT WITH ALMOND EGG PUFF

A golden egg batter covers succulent fish fillets for a fast oven entrée.

1-1/2 pounds turbot or sole fillets
1/2 teaspoon salt
paprika, pepper and onion powder to taste
1 tablespoon butter
4 eggs
1/4 cup sour cream
2 tablespoons mayonnaise
1/3 cup slivered blanched almonds

Arrange fish fillets close together in a buttered baking dish and sprinkle with salt, paprika, pepper and onion powder. Dot with butter. Place under the broiler and cook about 3 minutes to glaze the top. Beat together the eggs, sour cream and mayonnaise and spoon over fish. Sprinkle with almonds. Bake in a 375° oven for 15 to 20 minutes or until egg mixture puffs and is golden brown.
Makes 4 to 6 servings

SALMON AND ASPARAGUS MOUSSELINE

A beautiful spring combination: salmon, asparagus and new potatoes in a sophisticated version of hollandaise.

1 1-1/2-pound piece center-cut salmon
1/2 cup each dry white wine and fish stock or
   clam broth
1 slice lemon
1 pound small new potatoes
1-1/2 pounds asparagus
Mousseline Sauce, page 119

Poach the salmon in the wine and stock with the lemon slice just until tender, about 15 minutes, or until fish flakes with a fork. Meanwhile, cook potatoes in boiling salted water until tender, about 15 minutes; drain and keep warm. Break off tough ends of asparagus and cook spears in boiling salted water for 5 to 7 minutes or until tender; drain and keep warm. Prepare the Mousseline Sauce. Arrange on a platter the piece of salmon and surround with new potatoes and asparagus. Pass Mousseline Sauce to spoon over salmon and vegetables.
Makes 4 servings

MAYONNAISE

A blender speeds the task of making excellent homemade mayonnaise. It is important for the egg or egg yolks to be at room temperature when using either method.

2 egg yolks, if using classic method, or
1 egg, if using blender method
1 tablespoon freshly squeezed lemon juice
2 tablespoons white wine vinegar
1/2 teaspoon each salt, sugar and dry mustard
dash paprika
approximately 7/8 cup safflower oil

Classic method Place in a bowl the 2 egg yolks and beat for about 1 minute with a wire whisk or electric beater until thick. Add the lemon juice, vinegar, salt, sugar, mustard and paprika and beat 30 seconds longer. Gradually pour in the oil, drop by drop, beating constantly until thickened. Turn mayonnaise into a jar, cover and chill.
Blender method Place in the blender container the egg, lemon juice, vinegar, salt, sugar, mustard and paprika. Blend a few seconds. With blender turned on, gradually pour in the oil in a slow steady stream and blend until smooth and thickened. Turn mayonnaise into a jar, cover and chill.
Makes about 1 cup

AIOLI SAUCE

This Provencal garlic sauce provides a zestful dip for *crudités*. Or let it star at a supper, surrounded by large cooked shrimp, cherry tomatoes, mushroom caps and chilled cooked artichoke hearts or asparagus spears.

1 egg, at room temperature
3 tablespoons white wine vinegar
3/4 teaspoon salt
1 teaspoon Dijon-style mustard
3 or 4 large cloves garlic, chopped
1/4 cup olive oil
approximately 7/8 cup safflower oil

Place in a blender container the egg, vinegar, salt, mustard and garlic, and blend until smooth. With the motor running, gradually pour in the olive oil in a fine steady stream. Then slowly pour in the safflower oil, adding enough to make a thick mayonnaise consistency. Turn into a sauce bowl, cover and chill.
Makes about 1-1/4 cups

Eggy Entrees & Sauces

SKORDALIA SAUCE

The Greek add toasted pine nuts or almonds to garlic mayonnaise for a delightful accompaniment to broiled fish, cold cooked shrimp or lobster, or cold poached chicken breasts.

1 egg, at room temperature
3/4 teaspoon each salt and dry mustard
1-1/2 tablespoons each freshly squeezed
   lemon juice and white wine vinegar
3 cloves garlic, chopped
1/4 cup olive oil
approximately 3/4 cup safflower oil
1/4 cup finely chopped lightly toasted pine
   nuts or blanched almonds

Place in the blender container the egg, salt, mustard, lemon juice, vinegar and garlic, and blend a few seconds. With the motor running, slowly pour in the olive oil in a fine steady stream. Then slowly pour in the safflower oil, blending until thick. Add nuts and blend a second. Turn into a jar, cover and chill.
Makes about 1-1/4 cups

HOLLANDAISE SAUCE

This is a lovely sauce for sparking freshly cooked asparagus spears, broccoli, artichokes, poached salmon or lobster tails.

3 egg yolks
2 tablespoons freshly squeezed lemon juice
1/2 teaspoon grated lemon peel
1/4 teaspoon salt
approximately 1/4 pound butter

Classic method Beat egg yolks with a wire whisk about 1 minute in the top of a double boiler. Beat in lemon juice, lemon peel and salt until well blended. Melt butter until bubbly. Place yolk mixture over simmering water and gently beat in the melted butter in a slow steady stream, omitting the milky residue at the bottom of the butter pan and beating until thickened. Turn into a sauce bowl and keep warm in a pan of tepid water if not using immediately.
Blender method Rinse out the blender container with very hot water and drain. Put in the blender container the egg yolks, lemon juice, lemon peel and salt and blend a few seconds. Melt butter until bubbly. With motor running, gradually pour in butter in a slow steady stream, omitting the milky

residue at the bottom of the butter pan and blending just until smooth. Turn sauce into the top of a double boiler or a small saucepan and heat gently. Turn into a sauce bowl and keep warm in a pan of tepid water if not using immediately.
Makes about 1 cup

Note If sauce is not as thick as desired, add 2 or 3 tablespoons more melted butter. Leftover Hollandaise Sauce may be refrigerated 1 or 2 days, or frozen.

MOUSSELINE SAUCE

Fold 1/4 cup heavy cream, whipped, into 1 cup Hollandaise Sauce just before serving. Use as an accompaniment to fish, fish mousse or asparagus.

BÉARNAISE SAUCE

This is an exquisite companion to steak, prime rib, broiled fish or poached egg dishes.

1/4 cup white wine vinegar
2 tablespoons dry white wine or vermouth
1 shallot or green onion, chopped
1/2 teaspoon crumbled dried tarragon
1 sprig parsley
3 egg yolks
3/4 teaspoon Dijon-style mustard
3/4 cup butter

Classic method Place in a saucepan the vinegar, wine, shallot, tarragon and parsley. Cook over moderate heat until reduced to 2 tablespoons; strain and set aside. Beat egg yolks about 1 minute in the top of a double boiler with a wire whisk. Beat in the strained vinegar glaze and mustard and beat a few seconds. Melt the butter until bubbly. Place yolk mixture over simmering water and gently beat in the melted butter in a slow steady stream, omitting the milky residue at the bottom of the butter pan and beating until thickened. Turn into a sauce bowl and keep warm in a pan of tepid water if not using immediately.
Blender method Make vinegar glaze as directed in classic method. Rinse out a blender container with hot water and drain. Add egg yolks, strained vinegar glaze and mustard to blender container and blend a few seconds. Melt butter until bubbly. With motor running, slowly pour in butter in a fine steady stream, omitting the milky residue at the bottom of the butter pan and blending until thickened. Turn into a sauce bowl and keep warm in a pan of tepid water if not using immediately.
Makes about 1-1/4 cups

Note If available, 2 teaspoons minced fresh tarragon or 1/2 teaspoon crumbled dried tarragon makes a nice addition to stir in at the end.

Sweet Omelets Souffles & Custards

Sweet Omelets, Souffles & Custards

DESSERT OMELETS AND SOUFFLÉ OMELETS

For basic information on preparing omelets and soufflé omelets, see page 67.

NORWEGIAN OMELET

The origin of this confection is credited to a Chinese chef who visited Paris in the 1860's. He delighted guests at the Grand Hotel with his ginger and vanilla ices enveloped in hot meringue. The name is misleading; its other name, surprise omelet, is more appropriate. I've sampled some masterpieces in Paris which featured homemade strawberry ice and hazelnut and praline ice creams inside and were presented at tableside aflame with kirsch.

Sponge Cake, page 156
1 pint toasted almond ice cream
1 pint strawberry ice cream
2 tablespoons kirsch
4 egg whites
1/8 teaspoon each salt and cream of tartar
1/2 cup granulated sugar
2 egg yolks
1 teaspoon vanilla extract
powdered sugar

Prepare Sponge Cake as directed in recipe. Pack ice cream in layers into a round-bottomed bowl about 8 inches in diameter and freeze until firm. Place cake layer on a wooden board or ovenproof platter and drizzle it with kirsch. Unmold ice cream onto cake and place in the freezer while preparing the meringue. Beat egg whites until foamy, add salt and cream of tartar and beat until soft peaks form; gradually beat in granulated sugar 1 tablespoon at a time. Beat egg yolks until thick and lemon colored and beat in vanilla. Fold yolks into beaten whites. Spoon meringue over top and sides of ice cream-covered cake, covering it completely. Dust lightly with powdered sugar. Bake in a 500° oven for 3 to 4 minutes or until meringue is golden brown. Serve at once, cut in wedges.
Makes 6 to 8 servings

Sweet Omelets, Souffles & Custards

STRAWBERRIES IN CREAM OMELET

Fresh berries enveloped in whipped cream fill this hot puffy omelet that you flambé at the table.

2 eggs, separated
1/4 teaspoon salt
2 teaspoons granulated sugar
1 tablespoon butter
1 cup strawberries, sweetened to taste
1/2 cup heavy cream, whipped
powdered sugar
1 tablespoon kirsch

Beat egg whites and salt until soft peaks form. Beat egg yolks and granulated sugar until thick and light. Fold into the whites. Heat butter in an 8-inch omelet pan over medium-high heat; when it stops sizzling pour in the egg mixture. Cook until set. Combine strawberries and whipped cream and spoon into the middle of the omelet. Fold in half and turn out of pan. Dust the top with powdered sugar. At the table, ignite kirsch and spoon flaming over omelet.
Makes 2 servings

GLAZED APPLE SOUFFLÉ OMELET

Caramelized apple slices underlie this ethereal lemon-scented soufflé.

4 Golden Delicious apples or other cooking
    apples, peeled, cored and sliced
2 tablespoons butter
3/4 cup sugar
1 tablespoon freshly squeezed lemon juice
6 eggs, separated
1 teaspoon grated lemon peel
whipped cream or Almond Romanoff Sauce,
    page 127

In a large ovenproof frying pan, sauté apples over medium-high heat in butter with 1/4 cup of the sugar and the lemon juice until glazed, turning them frequently. Beat whites until soft peaks form. Add 1/4 cup of the sugar; beat until stiff. Beat yolks with remaining 1/4 cup sugar and lemon peel until thick and lemon colored. Fold in beaten egg whites. Spoon over the glazed apples and bake in a 375° oven for 15 to 20 minutes or until golden brown and set. Serve at once with whipped cream or Almond Romanoff Sauce.
Makes 6 servings

Sweet Omelets, Souffles & Custards

ORANGE SOUFFLÉ OMELET

Orange juice concentrate is the key to the zestful tang in this fluffy and quick dessert omelet.

6 eggs, separated
1/8 teaspoon salt
2/3 cup sugar
1/3 cup orange juice concentrate, thawed
1 tablespoon grated orange peel
2 tablespoons flour
2 tablespoons Grand Marnier or other
    orange-flavored liqueur (optional)
powdered sugar
whipped cream
sliced oranges, strawberries or raspberries

Beat egg whites with salt until soft peaks form; beat in sugar until stiff. Beat egg yolks until thick and lemon colored and beat in orange juice concentrate, orange peel, flour and liqueur. Fold in beaten egg whites. Spoon into a well-buttered 10-1/2-inch ovenproof frying pan and dust with powdered sugar. Bake in a 400° oven for 20 minutes or until golden brown. Serve with whipped cream and sliced orange or berries.
Makes 6 servings

LEMON SOUFFLÉ OMELET

A tangy lemon sauce blends beneath this light soufflé.

3 tablespoons butter
1/4 cup freshly squeezed lemon juice
3/4 cup sugar
6 eggs, separated
1/8 teaspoon salt
1 teaspoon grated lemon peel
1-1/2 pints toasted almond or vanilla ice cream

Melt butter in a 10-inch ovenproof baking dish or oval baking pan. Add lemon juice and 1/4 cup of the sugar and heat until dissolved. Tilt pan to coat with sauce. Beat egg whites with salt until soft peaks form. Add 1/4 cup of the sugar; beat until stiff. Beat egg yolks and lemon peel until thick and pale yellow and beat in remaining sugar. Fold in egg whites. Pile into coated pan. Bake in a 375° oven for 15 to 20 minutes or until golden brown and set. Serve with ice cream.
Makes 6 servings

Sweet Omelets, Souffles & Custards

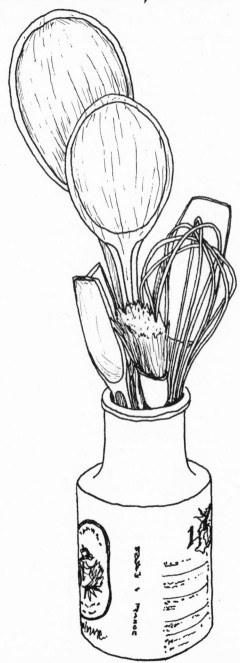

NUT CRUNCH SOUFFLÉ OMELET

Chocolate bits melt throughout this soufflé and caramelized almonds or filberts gild the bottom.

3 tablespoons each butter and sugar
6 tablespoons finely chopped almonds or filberts
6 eggs, separated
1/2 cup sugar
2 tablespoons rum
3 ounces (1/2 cup) semisweet chocolate bits
whipped cream or Romanoff Sauce, following

Melt butter and the 3 tablespoons sugar in a large ovenproof frying pan over medium heat. Add nuts and sauté until lightly toasted, stirring often. Remove from heat. Beat whites until soft peaks form. Add 1/4 cup of the sugar; beat until stiff. Beat yolks, remaining 1/4 cup sugar and rum until thick and lemon colored. Fold in beaten egg whites and chocolate bits. Spoon into the nut-crusted frying pan. Bake in a 375° oven for 15 to 20 minutes or until golden brown and set. Serve at once with whipped cream or Romanoff Sauce.
Makes 6 servings

Romanoff Sauce Whip 1/2 cup heavy cream until stiff, beat in 1 tablespoon rum or 1/2 teaspoon almond extract and 1 teaspoon vanilla extract. Add 1-1/2 pints vanilla or chocolate ice cream and beat until smoothly blended. Spoon into a freezer container and freeze until barely set, 15 minutes or longer.

Sweet Omelets, Souffles & Custards

DESSERT SOUFFLÉS

For basic information on preparing soufflés, see page 76.

SWEDISH SOUR CREAM SOUFFLÉ

This easy-to-assemble creamy soufflé is elegant accompanied with raspberries or strawberries and whipped cream.

6 eggs, separated
8 tablespoons sugar
dash salt
6 tablespoons sour cream
1 teaspoon grated lemon peel
fresh raspberries or strawberries, lightly sweetened
1 cup heavy cream, whipped and sweetened

Beat egg whites until soft peaks form and beat in 2 tablespoons of the sugar and the salt; beat until stiff. Beat egg yolks until light and add remaining sugar, beating well. Beat in sour cream and lemon peel and fold this mixture into the beaten egg whites. Spoon into a 10-inch round or oval baking dish. Bake in a 375° oven for 15 to 20 minutes or until golden brown and set. Serve at once accompanied with berries and whipped cream.
Makes 6 servings

HOT LEMON SOUFFLÉ

Drizzle a scarlet berry sauce and dollop puffs of cream on this zestful soufflé for a glorious dessert.

3/4 cup milk
2 tablespoons cornstarch
1/2 cup sugar
2 tablespoons butter
1/3 cup freshly squeezed lemon juice
2 teaspoons grated lemon peel
4 eggs, separated
2 egg whites
1/4 teaspoon each salt and cream of tartar
1 cup heavy cream, whipped and sweetened
1 10-ounce package frozen raspberries, thawed, puréed and strained to remove seeds

Blend 1/4 cup of the milk with cornstarch in a saucepan; stir in remaining milk and the sugar and cook over medium heat until thickened. Blend in butter, lemon juice, peel and egg yolks. Beat the 6 egg whites until foamy, add salt and cream of tartar and beat until stiff. Fold in the lemon mixture. Spoon into a buttered, sugared 1-1/2- to 2-quart baking dish and bake in a 375° oven for 30 to 35 minutes or until set. Serve at once with a bowl of whipped cream and pitcher of berry sauce to pour over.
Makes 6 to 8 servings

Sweet Omelets, Souffles & Custards

FILBERT PRALINE SOUFFLÉ

Crunchy nut candy jewels this airy soufflé. It is nice to know you can completely prepare this soufflé and let it stand up to an hour before baking. If your schedule demands earlier preparation, the alternative is to make the sauce ahead, refrigerate and reheat to lukewarm before folding in egg whites and baking.

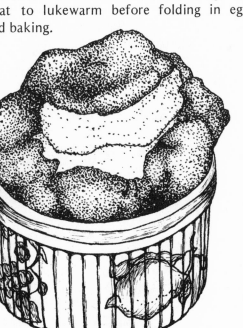

4 tablespoons butter
1/4 cup flour
1 cup milk
2/3 cup sugar
6 eggs, separated
1/4 cup dark rum
1/8 teaspoon each salt and cream of tartar
Praline, following
whipped cream for garnish (optional)

Place foil collar around a buttered 2-1/2-quart soufflé dish, see page 77. Sprinkle with sugar and shake out excess. Melt butter over medium heat in a saucepan and blend in flour; cook 2 minutes. Gradually stir in milk and 1/3 cup of the sugar. Cook, stirring, until sauce comes to a boil and boil 30 seconds. Remove from heat and beat in egg yolks one at a time. Stir in rum. Beat egg whites until foamy, add salt and cream of tartar and beat until soft peaks form. Beat in remaining sugar; continue beating until stiff. Fold whites and Praline into the sauce. Spoon into soufflé dish. Bake in a 375° oven for 40 minutes or until set. Serve at once with whipped cream if desired.
Makes 6 to 8 servings

Praline Place 6 tablespoons sugar in a heavy frying pan over moderate heat until sugar melts and turns amber. Add 6 tablespoons chopped filberts and shake to coat. Turn out on buttered foil; cool and chop finely.

COCONUT SOUFFLÉ

This heavenly hot soufflé is an apropos climax to a Spanish, Portuguese or Mexican meal. Like most other soufflés, it can be assembled up to one hour before slipping it into the oven.

3 tablespoons butter
1/4 cup flour
1 cup milk
6 tablespoons sugar
1 cup shredded coconut
4 eggs, separated
2 egg whites
1/2 teaspoon almond extract
2 teaspoons vanilla extract
Almond Romanoff Sauce, following

Melt butter in a saucepan over medium heat and blend in flour; cook, stirring, for 2 minutes. Gradually stir in milk and cook, stirring constantly, until thickened. Stir in 2 tablespoons of the sugar and the coconut. Cook, stirring, until sauce comes to a boil and boil 30 seconds. Remove from heat and beat in egg yolks one at a time. Set aside. Beat egg whites until soft peaks form and beat in remaining sugar and almond and vanilla extracts; beat until stiff. Fold into the coconut mixture. Turn into a well-buttered 2-quart oval baking dish or soufflé dish. Bake in a 375° oven for 35 to 40 minutes or until set and golden. Serve immediately with Almond Romanoff Sauce.
Makes 6 servings

Almond Romanoff Sauce Whip 1/2 cup heavy cream until stiff and beat in 1/2 teaspoon almond extract and 1-1/2 pints rich toasted almond ice cream. Beat just until smooth and fluffy. Turn into a freezer container and freeze until barely set but still mounding.

127

Sweet Omelets, Souffles & Custards

POOH'S HONEY SOUFFLÉ

Serve this ethereal dessert swiftly as its height is short-lived.

6 eggs, separated
1/4 teaspoon each salt and cream of tartar
2 tablespoons sugar
2/3 cup honey
1 teaspoon grated lemon peel
2 tablespoons each flour and melted butter
whipped cream (optional)
chocolate curls (optional)

Beat egg whites until foamy, add salt and cream of tartar and beat until soft peaks form. Add sugar and beat until stiff. Beat yolks until thick and lemon colored and beat in honey, lemon peel, flour and butter. Fold in whites. Spoon into a buttered 2-quart soufflé dish fitted with a foil collar (see page 77). Bake in a 375° oven for 30 to 35 minutes or until golden brown and set. Serve at once with whipped cream and chocolate curls, if desired.
Makes 6 servings

CHOCOLATE ALMOND SOUFFLÉ

This delectably rich chocolate soufflé is excellent baked in a large flat baking dish, such as a copper au gratin pan, for maximum crustiness.

6 ounces (1 cup) semisweet chocolate bits
6 eggs, separated
1/4 teaspoon each salt and cream of tartar
3/4 cup sugar
1/2 teaspoon almond extract
1/3 cup toasted chopped almonds
Romanoff Sauce, page 124

Heat chocolate in a small bowl over hot water until melted; let cool slightly. Beat egg whites until foamy, add salt and cream of tartar and beat until soft peaks form. Add 1/4 cup of the sugar; beat until stiff. Beat yolks until thick and pale yellow; beat in remaining sugar and almond extract. Stir in the melted chocolate and fold in the beaten egg whites and almonds. Heavily butter a 10-inch round baking dish and sprinkle with about 1 tablespoon sugar, just to coat surface. Spoon in the soufflé mixture. Bake in a 375° oven for 30 to 35 minutes or until set. Serve at once accompanied with Romanoff Sauce.
Makes 6 to 8 servings

Sweet Omelets, Souffles & Custards

CRÈME CARAMEL

This international dessert appears in infinite variation throughout Europe. The Danes fold the caramel syrup into whipped cream and use it to top the custard along with ice cream. The French flavor strawberries with kirsch and lace a custard ring with them. The Greeks layer a farina-strengthened custard between sheets of crispy fila pastry. And the Spanish scent their custard with citrus peel and ring it with fresh orange segments. This basic custard readily adapts to any of these variations.

1 cup sugar
3-1/2 cups milk (whole or extra-rich)
6 eggs
2 egg yolks
1 teaspoon vanilla extract
ice cream balls or whipped cream (optional)

Heat 1/2 cup of the sugar in a heavy saucepan until it melts and turns amber, shaking pan frequently. Immediately pour caramel into a 1-1/2-quart ring mold and tilt mold to coat all sides. Pour milk into the pan used to make the caramel and heat until scalding. Beat eggs and yolks until light and beat in remaining 1/2 cup sugar. Stir in scalded milk and vanilla extract. Pour into the caramel-lined mold, place in a pan of hot water and bake in a 350° oven for 50 minutes or until the custard is set. Let cool and chill. With a sharp-pointed knife, loosen custard from the mold and invert it on a large round platter. Accompany with ice cream balls or whipped cream, if desired.
Makes 8 servings

Variation For individual custards, pour hot caramel into 8 small custard cups (3/4-cup size). Prepare custard mixture as directed and pour into caramel-lined cups. Place cups in a pan of hot water and bake in a 350° oven for 30 minutes or until set.

CHEESE ROMANOFF

Scarlet raspberries lend a striking tart contrast to this creamy cheese pyramid.

1/4 pound butter, at room temperature
3/4 cup sugar
1 pound natural cream cheese, at room temperature
2 egg yolks
3/4 cup sour cream
2 teaspoons vanilla extract
fresh raspberries
1 10-ounce package frozen raspberries, puréed

Beat butter and sugar until creamy. Beat in cheese, egg yolks, sour cream and vanilla extract. Mound onto a platter and chill until firm. Garnish with berries and pass raspberry sauce to pour over.
Makes 12 servings

Sweet Omelets, Souffles & Custards

STRAWBERRIES WITH ITALIAN CUSTARD SAUCE

A sherried custard sauce smothers berries and ice cream for an ambrosial dessert.

4 egg yolks
6 tablespoons sugar
2 teaspoons cornstarch
3/4 cup pale dry sherry
1 teaspoon grated lemon peel
1 cup heavy cream
vanilla ice cream
2 cups strawberries, halved and sweetened to taste

Beat egg yolks, sugar and cornstarch in the top of a double boiler and stir in sherry. Cook, stirring over hot water until thickened; stir in lemon peel. Chill. Whip cream until thick and fold in. Spoon scoops of ice cream into dessert bowls and surround with berries. Spoon custard over.
Makes 6 to 8 servings

ORANGE CUSTARD-TOPPED FRUIT

Assorted seasonal fruits such as strawberries, fresh pineapple, seedless grapes and bananas make a refreshing dessert topped with a creamy orange custard sauce.

2 eggs, lightly beaten
1/3 cup sugar
1/3 cup orange juice
1 tablespoon freshly squeezed lemon juice
2 teaspoons grated orange peel
1 tablespoon butter, at room temperature
3/4 cup heavy cream
1 quart assorted sliced fruits (strawberries, pineapple, grapes, bananas, oranges)

In the top of a double boiler mix together the eggs, sugar, orange juice, lemon juice, orange peel and butter. Place over simmering water and cook until thickened, stirring constantly. Chill. Whip cream until stiff and fold in. Serve over bowls of fruit.
Makes 6 servings

RASPBERRY MACAROON MOUSSE

This gorgeous berry-pink frozen dessert is a fine choice for a party.

1-1/4 cups sugar
1/3 cup water
1 teaspoon light corn syrup
4 egg whites
2 10-ounce packages frozen raspberries, thawed
2 cups heavy cream
18 almond macaroons
2 to 3 tablespoons kirsch
fresh raspberries for garnish (optional)

Combine sugar, water and corn syrup in a small pan; bring to a boil and boil uncovered without stirring until the temperature reaches 238° (soft ball stage) on a candy thermometer. Meanwhile beat egg whites with an electric mixer until soft peaks form, then gradually beat in the hot syrup; continue beating at high speed until mixture cools to room temperature. Purée raspberries in a blender and press through a wire strainer, discarding seeds. Fold raspberry purée into the Italian meringue. Whip cream until stiff and fold in.

Spoon half the mousse mixture into a 9-inch spring-form pan. Dip macaroons quickly in kirsch to flavor them, and place a layer of macaroons on the raspberry mousse mixture. Cover with remaining raspberry mousse and arrange remaining liqueur-soaked macaroons in a design on top. Cover and freeze until firm, at least 8 hours. To serve, remove pan sides and cut in wedges. If desired, garnish with fresh raspberries.
Makes 12 servings

RIVOLI CHOCOLATE MOUSSE

This ultra-smooth, rich espresso-flavored chocolate mousse is a specialty of the Rivoli, a posh continental restaurant in Mexico City. Its charming Hungarian owner, Dario Bronzini, revealed its secret quartet of flavors: espresso, Kahlúa, chocolate and vanilla.

3 tablespoons water
2 teaspoons instant espresso
6 ounces semisweet chocolate
3 egg whites
1/4 cup sugar
1 cup heavy cream
1 tablespoon Kahlúa
1 teaspoon vanilla extract

In the top of a double boiler place the water, instant espresso and chocolate; heat over hot water until chocolate is melted; stir to blend and let cool to room temperature. Beat egg whites until soft peaks form and beat in sugar; beat until stiff. Whip cream until stiff and beat in Kahlúa and vanilla extract. Fold cream into cooled chocolate mixture and then fold in beaten egg whites. Spoon into small dessert bowls and chill.
Makes 8 servings

Sweet Omelets, Souffles & Custards

NATILLAS

In the Spanish version of "floating island," ribbons of caramel embellish the soft meringues, surrounded by custard.

6 eggs
1/8 teaspoon each salt and cream of tartar
1-1/3 cups sugar
2 tablespoons slivered blanched almonds
3 cups milk
2 teaspoons grated orange peel
1 teaspoon almond extract

Preheat oven to 425°. Separate 3 eggs. Beat the 3 whites until foamy, add salt and cream of tartar and beat until soft peaks form. Add 1/3 cup of the sugar; beat until stiff. Pour hot water 1 inch deep into a 9- by 13-inch baking pan and spoon 6 meringue balls onto the water. Sprinkle with almonds. Bake at 425° for 8 to 10 minutes or until browned. Remove from oven and lift meringues from water with a slotted spoon.

Heat milk until scalding and remove from heat. Beat the whole eggs and yolks until light and beat in 2/3 cup of the sugar. Stir in the hot milk. Pour into the top of a double boiler and heat over hot water, stirring constantly, until custard coats the spoon in a thick, velvety layer. Stir in orange peel and almond extract. Cool immediately in a pan of cold water. Pour into dessert bowls and chill. When ready to serve, place meringues on the custard. Melt remaining 1/3 cup sugar in a small, heavy frying pan until it turns amber and syrupy; immediately drizzle the hot sugar syrup over the meringues.
Makes 6 servings

CHAUDEAU

This foamy wine custard dessert is the German counterpart to the Italian zabaglione. Gewürztraminer, Johannisberg Riesling or Sylvaner may be substituted for the Rhine wine.

4 egg yolks
1/4 cup sugar
1 tablespoon brandy, Cointreau or Grand Marnier
1 teaspoon grated lemon peel
1 cup Rhine wine

In the top of a double boiler beat egg yolks until light; beat in sugar, brandy, lemon peel and wine. Place over simmering water and beat constantly with an electric beater or wire whisk. When very foamy and about tripled in volume pour into stemmed wineglasses and serve immediately.
Makes 4 servings

WINE SABAYON WITH BERRIES

A cherry brandy-flavored wine custard enhances raspberries and ice cream.

5 egg yolks
3 tablespoons sugar
1/2 cup dry white wine
3 tablespoons kirsch
1 pint toasted almond or vanilla ice cream
1-1/2 cups raspberries or hulled strawberries

In the top of a double boiler beat egg yolks and sugar until blended. Beat in wine. Beat over simmering water using a wire whisk or an electric beater until sauce is thick and custard-like. Remove from heat and stir in kirsch. Spoon ice cream and berries into dessert bowls and pour the wine custard over.

Makes 4 to 6 servings

Sweet Omelets, Souffles & Custards

FRENCH VANILLA ICE CREAM

A custard-based ice cream rich with egg yolks results in an ultra-smooth, elegant ice cream.

6 egg yolks
1-1/3 cups sugar
1 quart half-and-half
1/4 teaspoon salt
1 2-inch piece vanilla bean, split, or
2 tablespoons vanilla extract
2 cups heavy cream

Beat egg yolks slightly in the top of a double boiler and stir in sugar, half-and-half, salt and vanilla bean (if using vanilla extract, add it later). Place over simmering water and cook, stirring, until custard coats the spoon. Remove from heat and remove vanilla bean (or stir in vanilla extract). Chill.

Stir in heavy cream and pour into an ice cream freezer can, 1 gallon size. Place filled can in freezer pail and adjust dasher. Pack crushed ice and rock salt around can in proportions of 5 parts ice to 1 part salt. Churn using the crank or electric motor until ice cream is frozen, about 15 minutes. Remove dasher, scrape ice cream back into can and cover can. Drain off excess salt water and repack with ice and salt to hold until ready to serve.
Makes about 2-1/2 quarts

Coffee Ice Cream Follow the basic recipe for French Vanilla Ice Cream, using 1 tablespoon vanilla extract. In addition, dissolve 1/3 cup instant freeze-dried coffee in 3 tablespoons hot water. Stir into the basic custard mixture. Freeze as directed.

Nut Brittle Ice Cream Prepare the basic recipe for French Vanilla Ice Cream and stir 1-1/2 cups chopped nut brittle into the cool custard. Freeze as directed.

DUTCH LEMON CHIFFON

This delicate tart pudding is a refreshing finale to a hearty meal.

4 eggs, separated
1/2 cup plus 2 tablespoons sugar
1 teaspoon grated lemon peel
3 tablespoons freshly squeezed lemon juice
1/2 cup dry white wine

In the top of a double boiler beat egg yolks until light; beat in 1/2 cup of the sugar, lemon peel, lemon juice and wine. Place over hot water and cook until thickened, stirring constantly. Remove from heat. Beat egg whites until soft peaks form and beat in remaining 2 tablespoons sugar. Fold the hot lemon sauce into the meringue. Spoon into dessert dishes and chill.
Makes 6 servings

Sweet Omelets, Souffles & Custards

ALMOND CRUNCH SPUMONE

Caramelized nuts contribute an elegant contrast to this creamy liqueur-scented mousse. Accompany with fresh berries of the season.

2 teaspoons butter
1 cup plus 2 tablespoons sugar
1/2 cup chopped almonds or filberts
1/3 cup water
6 egg yolks
2 cups heavy cream
1/2 teaspoon almond extract
3 tablespoons kirsch
strawberries or raspberries for garnish

To make nut crunch, heat butter and 2 tablespoons of the sugar in a frying pan; add nuts and sauté, stirring until sugar melts and caramelizes and nuts are lightly toasted. Turn out of pan onto a sheet of buttered foil and let cool.

Combine remaining 1 cup sugar and water in a saucepan and bring to a boil. Boil until the temperature reaches 238° on a candy thermometer (soft ball stage). Meanwhile, beat egg yolks until thick and pale yellow. Continue beating yolks and immediately pour hot syrup over them in a fine stream. Beat until mixture cools to room temperature, about 7 minutes. Then chill until cold. Whip cream until stiff and flavor with almond extract and liqueur. Fold cream and 2/3 of the nut mixture into the yolks. Pour into a 2-quart mold, cover and freeze until firm, at least 8 hours.

Unmold by dipping mold in hot water. Turn out onto a platter and sprinkle with remaining nut crunch. Garnish with berries.
Makes 8 servings

Macaroon Spumone Omit nut crunch. Sprinkle 3/4 cup crumbled almond macaroons with 2 tablespoons kirsch or maraschino liqueur and substitute 3 tablespoons Grand Marnier or other orange-flavored liqueur for the 3 tablespoons kirsch.

Strawberry Bombe Pack 1 quart strawberry ice or raspberry sherbet into a 2-1/2-quart salad mold or brioche mold, making a layer about 3/4 inch thick on the bottom and sides. Freeze until firm. Prepare 1 recipe Almond Crunch Spumone and spoon into the sherbet-lined mold. Cover and freeze until firm, about 8 hours. Unmold by dipping mold in very hot water and turning out onto a platter. Return to the freezer for about 10 minutes to firm up. Cut in wedges. Makes 12 servings.

Chocolate Bombe Pack 1 quart chocolate ice cream into a 2-1/2-quart salad mold or brioche mold, making a layer about 3/4 inch thick on the bottom and sides. Freeze until firm. Prepare 1 recipe Almond Crunch Spumone substituting rum for the kirsch. Spoon into the ice cream-lined mold. Cover and freeze until firm, about 8 hours. Unmold as directed above. Makes 12 servings.

Dessert Crepes
Egg Pastries

DESSERT CRÊPES

A bit of liqueur lends a pleasant subtlety to faintly sweet crêpes. For basic instructions on preparing crêpes, see page 98.

1 cup milk
3 eggs
3/4 cup all-purpose flour
2 teaspoons sugar
1 tablespoon rum, brandy or orange-flavored
   liqueur
butter as needed

In a blender container place the milk, eggs, flour, sugar and liquor. Or place in a mixing bowl and beat with a wire whisk. Blend until smooth. Let batter stand at least 30 minutes. Heat a 6-inch crêpe pan over medium heat, add 1/2 to 1 teaspoon butter and tilt pan to coat surface. Pour in just enough batter to coat pan (about 2 tablespoons) and tilt pan to cover surface. Cook until golden brown on the edges and dry on top. Turn out onto a plate. Repeat with remaining batter, adding butter as needed. Stack crêpes and use in the following ways or refrigerate.
Makes about 16 crêpes

Lemon Angel Crêpes Prepare the lemon filling of Lemon Angel Pie, page 144. Fill crêpes, roll and top with whipped cream flavored with Cointreau.

Chocolate Mousse Crêpes Fill crêpes with Rivoli Chocolate Mousse, page 131. Roll and top with whipped cream.

Nut Soufflé Crêpes Fill crêpes with unbaked Filbert Praline Soufflé, page 126. Fold loosely into envelopes and bake at 375° for 20 to 25 minutes or until puffed and golden.

Orange Custard Crêpes Prepare custard for Orange Custard-Topped Fruit, page 130. Fill crêpes with custard, garnish with mandarin oranges or orange segments and sprinkle with toasted slivered almonds.

Mincemeat-Apple Crêpes Flambé Fill crêpes with mincemeat blended with diced apple sautéed in butter until soft. Roll and bake at 375° for 10 to 15 minutes or until hot through. Flame with brandy or Cognac.

Raspberries and Cream Crêpes Fill crêpes with whipped cream flavored with kirsch and raspberries or blueberries. Roll and serve with a sauce of puréed raspberries, sweetened to taste (or thawed frozen raspberries, puréed and sieved).

Honey-Butter Crêpes Beat 5 tablespoons butter until creamy and beat in 1/3 cup honey, beating until smooth. Drop a spoonful on each crêpe and roll up.

Cinnamon-Sugar Crêpes Dust each crêpe with a mixture of cinnamon and sugar and roll up. Place in a baking pan, dot with butter, sprinkle with sugar and slip under the broiler until browned.

Dessert Crepes & Egg Pastries

ICE CREAM SUNDAE CRÊPES

12 Dessert Crêpes, page 137
4 ounces semisweet chocolate
1/4 cup each light corn syrup and coffee
1/2 teaspoon almond extract
1 pint coffee or toasted almond ice cream

Prepare crêpes as directed in recipe. Then make a chocolate sauce by melting chocolate with corn syrup and coffee over hot water; stir until thickened. Stir in almond extract. Place a heaping tablespoon of ice cream in each crêpe and roll up. Pour hot chocolate sauce over crêpes.
Makes 4 to 6 servings

CHOCOLATE ALMOND CRÊPES

16 Dessert Crêpes, page 137
3/4 cup chopped almonds or filberts
1 tablespoon butter
6 tablespoons sugar
2 cups grated semisweet chocolate
2 tablespoons butter, melted
whipped cream flavored with rum or brandy

Prepare crêpes as directed in recipe. In a frying pan sauté the nuts in the 1 tablespoon butter and 2 tablespoons of the sugar until caramelized and lightly toasted. Let cool. Mix together the caramelized nuts and chocolate and sprinkle each crêpe with about 3 tablespoons of the chocolate-nut mixture. Fold like an envelope and place in a buttered baking dish. Sprinkle with remaining 4 tablespoons sugar and the melted butter. Bake in a 400° oven for 10 minutes or until heated through. Serve with flavored whipped cream.
Makes 6 to 8 servings

Dessert Crepes & Egg Pastries

HACIENDA CRÊPES SUZETTES

The elegant Hacienda de Morales in Mexico City makes a flourish of these dessert crêpes, each beautifully imbued with citrus.

12 Dessert Crêpes, page 137
1/4 cup sugar
1 strip each orange and lime peels*
2 tablespoons each butter and
    freshly squeezed lime juice
1 cup orange juice
2 tablespoons each Cointreau, Cognac and
    Grand Marnier

Prepare crêpes as directed in recipe. In a chafing dish or frying pan heat sugar with orange and lime peels until sugar melts and turns amber. Add butter, lime juice and orange juice and heat, stirring until blended. Fold crêpes in quarters and arrange crêpe triangles in an overlapping circle in the pan. Combine the liqueurs, ignite and spoon flaming over the crêpes. Serve immediately by placing 3 crêpes on each dish and pouring flaming sauce over.
Makes 4 servings

*This is most easily done by using a vegetable peeler to make a 1/2-inch-wide strip from top to bottom of fruit.

STRAWBERRY CUSTARD CRÊPES

16 Dessert Crêpes, page 137
3 egg yolks
2/3 cup granulated sugar
4 teaspoons cornstarch
3/4 cup milk
3/4 cup heavy cream
1 tablespoon orange-flavored liqueur
2-1/2 cups strawberries, hulled
powdered sugar

Prepare crêpes as directed in recipe. Beat together the egg yolks, granulated sugar and cornstarch; stir in milk. Cook in the top of a double boiler until thickened. Chill. Whip cream until stiff and beat in liqueur; fold whipped cream into the custard sauce. Set aside 1/2 cup whole berries for garnish. Slice remaining berries in half and sweeten to taste. Mix sliced berries into custard. Spoon a mound on the center of each crêpe and roll up. Garnish each with 1 or 2 berries and dust with powdered sugar.
Makes 8 servings

Dessert Crepes & Egg Pastries

ELEGANT CHEESECAKE

Here is a beautiful party-size cheesecake from a superb Jewish cook. Plan to bake it a day in advance so its creamy consistency has a chance to set up.

Graham Cracker Crust, following
8 eggs, separated
1-1/2 cups granulated sugar
4 8-ounce packages cream cheese, at
    room temperature
3 tablespoons freshly squeezed lemon juice
2 teaspoons grated lemon peel
1 cup (1/2 pint) sour cream
2 teaspoons powdered sugar
1 teaspoon vanilla extract

Prepare crust as directed below. Beat egg yolks until thick and pale and beat in granulated sugar gradually. Slowly beat in cheese. Add lemon juice and peel. Beat egg whites until stiff but not dry and fold in. Turn into the crust-lined spring-form pan. Bake in a 350° oven for 45 minutes or until barely set. Remove from oven and turn up heat to 400°. Combine sour cream, powdered sugar and vanilla extract and spread on top. Bake at 400° for 5 minutes. Turn off oven, open oven door, and let cool to room temperature. Then cover and refrigerate overnight.
Makes about 16 servings

Graham Cracker Crust Combine 1 cup crushed graham cracker crumbs, 2 tablespoons melted butter and 1 tablespoon sugar and pat into the bottom and part way up the sides of a 10-inch spring-form pan. Bake at 325° for 8 minutes.

SOUR CREAM SOUFFLÉ CHEESECAKE

Baked without a crust, this cheesecake resembles a snowy cheese soufflé. Fresh strawberries or raspberries can enhance it.

1 pound cream cheese

6 eggs, separated

1 cup sugar

1-1/2 cups (12 ounces) sour cream

3 tablespoons freshly squeezed lemon juice

1 teaspoon vanilla extract

1/4 cup flour

Let all ingredients come to room temperature. Beat cheese until creamy and beat in egg yolks one at a time. Gradually beat in sugar, sour cream, lemon juice, vanilla extract and flour. Beat egg whites until stiff but not dry; fold into creamed mixture. Turn into a buttered 10-inch spring-form pan. Bake in a 325° oven for 1 hour. Turn off oven and let stand in the unopened oven 1 hour. Open oven door and let stand 30 minutes longer. Remove from oven, let cool and then chill. Remove pan sides and place on a platter to serve.
Makes 12 servings

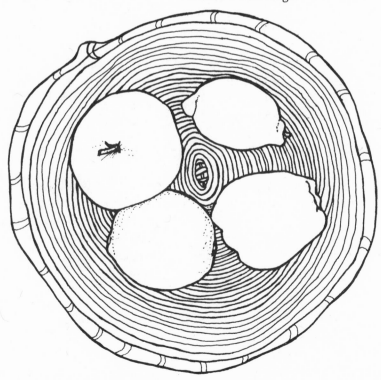

Dessert Crepes & Egg Pastries

NATURAL CREAM CHEESECAKE

A 2-pound carton of natural cream cheese (without emulsifiers) is the basis for this supremely simple party cheesecake. Vary the topping to suit the fruit in season.

2 pounds natural cream cheese, at room
   temperature
1-1/3 cups sugar
6 eggs
3/4 teaspoon almond extract
1 teaspoon vanilla extract
fruit topping of sliced strawberries, sugared
   raspberries or canned cherry pie filling (optional)

Place cheese in a mixing bowl and beat until creamy. Gradually add sugar and beat until smooth. Beat in eggs and almond and vanilla extracts. Pour into a well-buttered 9- or 10-inch spring-form pan. Bake in a 325° oven for 40 minutes or until set. Let cool at room temperature, then chill overnight. To serve, remove pan sides, cut in wedges and garnish with fruit topping if desired.
Makes 12 servings

CHOCOLATE MARBLE CHEESECAKE

Melted chocolate swirls through this creamy cheesecake, punctuating it with richness.

Zweiback Crust, following
1 pound cream cheese, at room temperature
3 eggs
3/4 cup sugar
1 teaspoon vanilla extract
3 ounces semisweet chocolate, melted

Prepare crust as directed below. To make filling beat cheese until creamy and mix in eggs, sugar and vanilla extract. Pour filling into the baked crust. Drizzle melted chocolate over the filling and with a fork gently swirl chocolate into the cheese mixture. Bake in a 350° oven for 25 minutes or until set. Let cool and chill. To serve remove pan sides and cut in wedges.
Makes 8 to 10 servings

Zweiback Crust Mix together 1 cup crushed zwieback or graham cracker crumbs, 3 tablespoons melted butter and 2 tablespoons sugar. Pat into the bottom and part way up the sides of a 9-inch spring-form pan. Bake in a 325° oven for 8 minutes.

HONEYMOON SPECIAL LEMON PIE

This refreshing soufflé-like lemon pie is a perfect finale to almost any meal.

Sweet Butter Crust I, following
8 eggs, separated
1-1/2 cups sugar
1/2 cup freshly squeezed lemon juice
1 teaspoon grated lemon peel
3 tablespoons butter, at room temperature
1/4 teaspoon each salt and cream of tartar

Prepare Sweet Butter Crust as directed below. Beat egg yolks until light and beat in 3/4 cup of the sugar, lemon juice, lemon peel and butter. Pour into the top of a double boiler and cook, stirring constantly, until thickened. Beat egg whites until foamy, add salt and cream of tartar and beat until stiff; gradually beat in remaining 3/4 cup sugar. Fold half of the egg-white mixture into the cooked lemon sauce. Spoon into the baked shell. Spread remaining meringue on top, covering completely. Bake in a 325° oven for 35 minutes or until well browned. Let cool and remove from pan.
Makes 10 to 12 servings

Sweet Butter Crust I In a mixing bowl combine 1 cup all-purpose flour, 2 tablespoons powdered sugar and 1/2 cup butter. Beat until crumbly and press into bottom and sides of a 10- or 11-inch fluted flan pan with removable bottom. Bake at 425° for 8 minutes.

FRENCH PEAR PIE

A soufflé-like cake binds together this pretty open-face fruit tart.

Sweet Butter Crust II, following
6 cooking pears (Bartlett, Anjou or Bosc)
2 eggs
1 cup sugar
2 tablespoons butter, melted
2 tablespoons heavy cream
1 teaspoon vanilla extract
1/2 teaspoon grated lemon peel, or
1/8 teaspoon ground mace
3 tablespoons flour

Prepare Butter Crust as directed below. Peel and slice pears and arrange in crust-lined pan. Beat eggs until thick and pale in color and beat in sugar. Add butter, cream, vanilla extract, lemon peel and flour and blend well. Pour over pears. Sprinkle with remaining crumbs from crust. Bake at 425° for 15 minutes, then at 400° for 25 minutes or until set and golden brown.
Makes 8 servings

Sweet Butter Crust II Mix together 1/4 pound butter and 1-1/3 cups flour until crumbly; mix in 1 egg. Reserve 1/2 cup crumbs and pat remainder into the bottom and sides of a 10- or 11-inch flan pan with removable bottom or a 9-inch pie pan.

Dessert Crepes & Egg Pastries

LEMON ANGEL PIE

This old-fashioned lemon meringue torte gains a new dimension with the tang of sour cream.

6 eggs, separated
1/4 teaspoon cream of tartar
1-1/4 cups sugar
1/2 cup freshly squeezed lemon juice
3/4 cup heavy cream
1/3 cup sour cream

Beat egg whites until foamy; add cream of tartar and beat until soft peaks form. Gradually beat in 3/4 cup of the sugar, beating until stiff. Spoon into bottom and sides of a buttered 10-inch spring-form pan. Bake in a 300° oven 45 minutes; cool. Beat egg yolks in the top of a double boiler and beat in remaining sugar and the lemon juice. Cook, stirring, over hot water until thickened; cool. Whip cream until stiff and beat in sour cream. Spread half of the cream mixture in the cool meringue shell. Cover with lemon filling and spoon remaining cream on top. Chill at least 4 hours.
Makes 8 servings

BAKED ALASKA PIE

A golden brown meringue topping seals in the frosty ice cream filling of this novel pie.

1-1/4 cups crushed graham cracker crumbs
4 tablespoons butter, melted
2 tablespoons brown sugar
1 quart butter brickle ice cream
4 egg whites
1/8 teaspoon each salt and cream of tartar
1 cup sugar

Mix together the crumbs, butter and brown sugar and pat into the bottom and sides of a 9-inch pie pan. Bake in a 325° oven for 8 to 10 minutes. Let cool. Pack ice cream into the shell and place in the freezer.

A few hours before serving, beat egg whites until foamy, add salt and cream of tartar and beat until soft peaks form. Gradually beat in the sugar, beating until stiff. Swirl meringue over the top of the pie, sealing the edges. Bake in a 450° oven for 5 to 6 minutes or until the top is golden brown. Return to the freezer until serving time. May be frozen up to 2 days.
Makes 8 servings

"Mud Pie" Variation Substitute chocolate cookie crumbs and coffee or peppermint ice cream for the graham cracker crumbs and butter brickle ice cream. Spread 1/2 cup canned chocolate syrup or homemade chocolate sauce (see Ice Cream Sundae Crêpes, page 138) over the ice cream-lined pie before topping with meringue.

Dessert Crepes & Egg Pastries

BLACK BOTTOM RUM PIE

A chocolate frosting coats the pastry of this fluffy rum-flavored Bavarian cream pie.

Butter-Nut Crust, following
Chocolate Glaze, following
1 envelope unflavored gelatin
1/4 cup cold water
1/3 cup rum
4 eggs, separated
3/4 cup sugar
3/4 cup heavy cream
semisweet chocolate curls

Prepare crust as directed below and spread baked shell with Chocolate Glaze. Sprinkle gelatin into cold water and let stand until softened; place over hot water and let stand until dissolved; stir in rum. Beat whites until soft peaks form; beat in half of the sugar (6 tablespoons); beat until stiff. Beat egg yolks until thick and pale in color and beat in remaining sugar. Then mix in the gelatin-rum liquid. Fold in beaten egg whites. Whip cream until stiff and fold in. Spoon into the chocolate-covered pastry shell and chill until set. Garnish with chocolate curls.
Makes 10 servings

Butter-Nut Crust Combine 1 cup flour, 3 tablespoons very finely chopped toasted almonds or filberts, 2 tablespoons powdered sugar and 1/4 pound butter. Press into the bottom and sides of an 11-inch flan pan (with removable bottom) or a 9-inch pie pan. Bake at 425° for 8 minutes or until golden brown.

Chocolate Glaze Beat 3 tablespoons butter and 1/4 cup powdered sugar until blended. Mix in 2 ounces melted semisweet chocolate.

Dessert Crepes & Egg Pastries

RUM PRALINE CREAM PUFF

Here is a star-shaped gala dessert for the holiday season.

1 cup water
1/8 teaspoon salt
1/4 pound butter
1 cup all-purpose flour
4 eggs
Rum Cream Filling, following
1/3 cup sugar
3 tablespoons slivered toasted almonds

In a saucepan place the water, salt and butter; heat until butter melts. Bring to a full rolling boil, add flour all at once, remove from heat and beat until paste leaves sides of the pan. Add eggs, one at a time, beating until smooth. Spoon paste into a pastry bag with a star tip and press out onto a greased baking sheet into a 5- or 6-pointed star shape about 12 inches across. Bake in a 400° oven for 20 minutes; reduce heat to 375° and bake 30 minutes longer; let cool on a rack. To serve, split shell and fill with Rum Cream Filling. Heat sugar until it melts and turns amber and dribble caramel over puff; sprinkle with almonds and chill.
Makes 12 servings

Rum Cream Filling Stir together in the top of a double boiler 2/3 cup sugar, 2 teaspoons unflavored gelatin, 1/8 teaspoon salt and 1-1/4 cups milk. Place over hot water and heat until scalded. Beat 4 egg yolks until light and blend in milk mixture; return to double boiler and cook until thickened. Cool and stir in 2 tablespoons rum. Whip 1 cup heavy cream until stiff and fold in.

Tortes, Cakes & Cookies

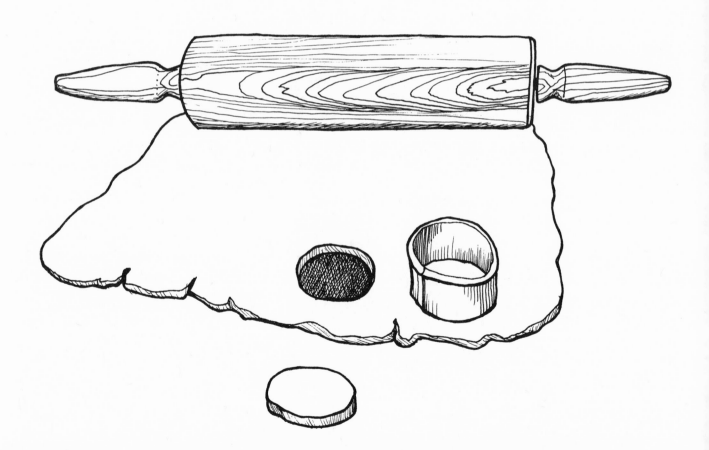

LINZER TORTE

A winning Viennese trio of flavors—almonds, raspberries and chocolate—intertwine in this elegant dessert torte.

1/2 pound butter
1 cup sugar
2 eggs
1 teaspoon grated lemon peel
1-1/2 cups all-purpose flour
1 cup unblanched almonds, ground
1/2 teaspoon each ground cinnamon and cloves
1 tablespoon unsweetened powdered cocoa
1/4 teaspoon salt
1-1/2 cups raspberry jam
whipped cream
semisweet chocolate curls

Beat butter and sugar until creamy. Add eggs and lemon peel and beat until blended. Stir together the flour, almonds, cinnamon, cloves, cocoa and salt. Add dry ingredients to creamed mixture and mix until smooth. Form into a ball and chill slightly. Break off 1/4 of the dough and reserve for lattice topping. Roll out remaining dough on a lightly floured board into a circle about 1/4 inch thick and line a 9-inch pie pan. Fill pan with jam and roll remaining dough into strips and make a lattice design on top. Flute the edge. Bake in a 300° oven for 1 hour. Let cool. Serve with a bowl of whipped cream garnished with chocolate curls. Makes 8 servings

FILBERT MERINGUE TORTE WITH APRICOT CREAM

This pretty Austrian torte has a refreshing apricot filling sandwiched between crispy nut meringue.

6 egg whites
1 teaspoon white distilled vinegar
1/8 teaspoon salt
1-1/2 cups sugar
1 cup ground filberts, lightly toasted
1 cup dried apricots
sliver of lemon peel
1 cup water
1 cup heavy cream
8 to 10 whole filberts for garnish

Beat egg whites until foamy, add vinegar and salt and beat until soft peaks form. Gradually beat in sugar, beating until stiff and glossy. Fold in ground nuts. Butter 2 9-inch round baking pans and line with waxed paper; butter paper and dust with flour. Spread meringue in pans. Bake in a 375° oven for 30 to 35 minutes. Remove from pans and peel off paper.

Cook apricots with lemon peel and water until tender, about 15 minutes. Let cool, purée in a blender and sweeten to taste. Whip cream until stiff and fold half of it into the apricot purée. Spread on one meringue layer; top with other layer. Spoon remaining cream on top and garnish with whole nuts. Chill several hours. Cut in wedges. Makes 12 servings

Tortes, Cakes & Cookies

CHOCOLATE SAND TORTE

Slice this rich chocolate pound cake thinly and serve with strawberries, pears, peaches or other fresh fruit.

1/2 pound butter
2-1/2 cups sugar
5 eggs
1/2 teaspoon almond extract
1/2 cup sour cream
3 cups all-purpose flour
1/2 teaspoon each salt and baking powder
1 teaspoon baking soda
1/2 cup unsweetened powdered cocoa

Beat butter and sugar until creamy and beat in eggs one at a time. Add almond extract and sour cream. Stir together flour, salt, baking powder, baking soda and cocoa and blend the dry ingredients into creamed mixture. Turn into a buttered and floured bundt pan or 10-inch tube pan. Bake in a 325° oven for 1 hour and 40 minutes or until a toothpick inserted in center comes out clean. Let cool on a rack, then turn out of pan.
Makes about 16 servings

CHOCOLATE-RUM LADYFINGER TORTE

A party dessert to make ahead, this torte is enhanced by bitefuls of rum-soaked macaroons.

1 12-ounce package semisweet chocolate bits
1/4 cup strong coffee (2 teaspoons instant coffee blended with 2 tablespoons water)
6 eggs, separated
1/4 pound butter, at room temperature
1 teaspoon vanilla extract
1/3 cup sugar
1-1/4 cups heavy cream
1 3-ounce package ladyfingers (24 split ladyfingers)
3/4 cup coarsely crumbled almond macaroons (approximately 6 cookies)
3 tablespoons rum
1/4 cup toasted chopped almonds

Melt chocolate with coffee in a bowl over hot water. Remove from heat and beat in egg yolks one at a time. Beat in soft butter and vanilla extract; cool to room temperature. Beat egg whites until stiff and beat in sugar. Fold meringue into cooled chocolate mixture. Beat cream until stiff and fold in. Stand split ladyfingers around the sides of a 9-inch spring-form pan and spoon in half the chocolate filling. Soak the macaroon bits in rum and sprinkle on top of filling with half the nuts. Top with remaining filling, cover and chill. Just before serving, sprinkle remaining nuts on top.
Makes 12 to 14 servings

CHOCOLATE FILBERT TORTE

This elegant Viennese nut torte is a grand party dessert to make in advance.

6 ounces semisweet chocolate
2 cups ground filberts or pecans
2 tablespoons flour
3/4 cup each butter and sugar
6 eggs, separated
1/2 cup raspberry jelly or puréed apricot jam
Chocolate Buttercream, following

Melt chocolate slowly over hot water and let cool to room temperature. Mix nuts with flour. Beat butter and sugar until creamy and beat in egg yolks. Stir in melted chocolate and the nut mixture. Beat egg whites until stiff and fold in. Pour into a buttered and floured 10-inch spring-form pan and bake in a 350° oven for 30 minutes or until a toothpick inserted in center comes out clean. Let cool on a rack. Remove pan sides and spread top with raspberry jelly or puréed apricot jam, slightly melted. Make Chocolate Buttercream and spread on top and sides of cake when jelly or jam has set. Chill.
Makes 12 servings

Chocolate Buttercream Melt 4 ounces semisweet chocolate over hot water; let cool. Beat 4 tablespoons butter and 1/2 cup powdered sugar until blended and mix in 2 egg yolks and 1/2 teaspoon vanilla extract. Stir in melted chocolate.

ITALIAN CRUNCH TORTE

A nut-filled meringue makes a delectable base to top with strawberries, nectarines or peaches and whipped cream.

4 egg whites
1/4 teaspoon each cream of tartar and salt
1 cup sugar
3/4 cup crushed graham cracker crumbs
  (6 double crackers)
1/2 cup each walnuts and almonds, ground
1-1/2 cups berries or other fresh fruit
1/2 cup heavy cream, whipped and flavored
  with vanilla extract

Beat egg whites until foamy, add salt and cream of tartar and beat until stiff. Gradually beat in sugar in a slow steady stream and beat until smooth and glossy. Fold in crumbs and nuts. Turn into a buttered 9- or 10-inch spring-form pan and bake in a 375° oven for 25 minutes or until set and slightly browned on the edges. Let cool; then cut in wedges and top with fruit and whipped cream.
Makes 6 servings

Tortes, Cakes & Cookies

ORANGE-FILLED SCHAUM TORTE

Make the meringue shell for this party refrigerator dessert days in advance if you wish, but plan to fill it early the day you serve it.

5 egg whites
1/4 teaspoon each salt and cream of tartar
1-3/4 cups granulated sugar
1 teaspoon vanilla extract
2 cups orange juice
1/4 cup cornstarch blended with
    1/2 cup cold water
2 eggs, beaten
1 teaspoon each grated orange and lemon peel
1 tablespoon freshly squeezed lemon juice
1-1/2 cups heavy cream
1 teaspoon vanilla extract
1-1/2 tablespoons powdered sugar
grated semisweet chocolate

Beat egg whites until foamy. Add salt and cream of tartar and beat until stiff. Gradually beat in 1-1/4 cups of the sugar, beating until thick and glossy. Beat in vanilla extract. Spread on the bottom and sides of a buttered 10-inch spring-form pan. Bake at 300° for 1 hour until lightly browned and dry.

Heat orange juice with remaining 1/2 cup sugar and bring to a boil. Blend in cornstarch paste and cook until thickened. Stir part of the sauce into the beaten eggs and return mixture to the pan; cook until thickened. Add grated peels and lemon juice. Cool and chill.

The day torte is to be served, whip cream and flavor with vanilla extract and powdered sugar. Spread two-thirds of cream over cool shell. Cover with orange filling. Chill. To serve, decorate with remaining whipped cream, spooned in dollops on top, and grated chocolate.
Serves 8 to 10

SERBIAN MERINGUE TORTE

Present this nutty meringue torte warm to savor the melting chocolate streaks.

4 egg whites
1/8 teaspoon salt
1/4 cup sugar
1/4 cup orange marmalade
3/4 cup ground almonds or filberts
2 ounces semisweet chocolate, grated
ice cream or Romanoff Sauce, page 124

Beat egg whites and salt until soft peaks form; beat in sugar, beating until stiff. Beat in orange marmalade. Fold in nuts and chocolate. Spoon into a buttered 9-inch round pan. Place in a pan of hot water. Bake in a 300° oven for 1 hour. Serve warm, preferably, or at room temperature with ice cream or Romanoff Sauce.
Makes 6 servings

Tortes, Cakes & Cookies

STRAWBERRY CUSTARD TORTE

This gala, berry-bedecked layer torte is easily made ahead of time.

3 eggs
1-1/2 cups sugar
1-1/2 teaspoons vanilla extract
3/4 cup milk
3 tablespoons butter
1-1/2 cups all-purpose flour
1-1/2 teaspoons baking powder
1/2 teaspoon salt
Custard Filling, following
1/2 cup raspberry jelly or strawberry jam
2 cups strawberries, hulled
toasted sliced almonds for garnish

Beat eggs until thick; beat in sugar and vanilla extract. Heat milk and butter until butter melts; set aside. Stir together flour, baking powder and salt and mix into the egg mixture. Stir in milk mixture. Pour into a buttered and floured 9-inch spring-form pan. Bake in a 350° oven for 40 to 45 minutes or until a toothpick inserted in center comes out clean. Let cool on a rack, then remove pan sides.

Prepare Custard Filling as directed below. Split cake into 2 layers; spread one layer with filling and top with other half. Heat jelly or jam until melted and spread half on the top layer. Stand berries upright on top of torte. Spread remaining jelly around sides and sprinkle with nuts. Chill until serving time.
Makes 10 servings

Custard Filling In a blender container place 1-1/2 cups milk, 3 tablespoons cornstarch, 1/4 teaspoon salt, 1/2 cup sugar and 4 egg yolks. Blend until smooth. Pour into the top of a double boiler, place over hot water and cook, stirring, until thickened. Add 1 teaspoon vanilla extract and 1 tablespoon butter and let cool. Whip 1/2 cup heavy cream until stiff and beat in 1 tablespoon each brandy or Cognac and orange-flavored liqueur. Fold whipped cream into cooled custard.

COFFEE BUTTERCREAM TORTE

This exemplifies the elegant tortes of Vienna.

Sponge Cake, page 156
1/4 cup granulated sugar
2 tablespoons water
3 tablespoons rum
1/2 cup puréed apricot jam
3/4 cup butter
2 egg yolks
1-1/2 cups powdered sugar
2 tablespoons very strong coffee (2 teaspoons instant coffee blended with
    2 tablespoons water)
1 teaspoon vanilla extract
1/4 cup slivered toasted almonds

Prepare Sponge Cake as directed in recipe; set aside to cool. When cool slice horizontally into 2 9-inch rounds. Meanwhile combine granulated sugar and water in a saucepan, bring to a boil and cook without stirring until clear; stir in 2 tablespoons of the rum. Drizzle syrup over both cake layers and let cool. Boil jam with remaining 1 tablespoon rum until slightly reduced; spread on top of one layer and place the other layer on top.

In a mixing bowl place the butter, egg yolks, powdered sugar, coffee and vanilla extract. Let ingredients come to room temperature; then beat until blended. Spread over top and sides of cake. Sprinkle top of cake with almonds. Chill until set.
Makes 12 servings

DÉLICE AU CHOCOLATE

This chocolate torte resembles a wonderful chocolate brownie, soufflé-like in character.

12 ounces semisweet chocolate
6 eggs, separated
1 tablespoon dark rum, or
1 teaspoon vanilla extract
4 tablespoons sugar
2 tablespoons flour
1/4 teaspoon salt
1/4 pound butter, at room temperature
Romanoff Sauce, page 124, or rich
    vanilla ice cream

Place chocolate in a small pan and heat in a 300° oven for 10 minutes or until chocolate is melted; let cool slightly. Beat egg yolks until light and beat in rum, 1 tablespoon of the sugar, flour, salt and butter. Stir in chocolate and mix until smooth. Beat egg whites until soft peaks form and beat in remaining 3 tablespoons sugar; beat until stiff. Fold beaten whites into chocolate mixture. Turn into a buttered 9-inch spring-form pan. Bake in a 400° oven for 20 to 25 minutes or until the center is barely firm when touched lightly. Let cool, then chill. Cut into wedges and serve with Romanoff Sauce or rich vanilla ice cream.
Makes 12 servings

Tortes, Cakes & Cookies

SPONGE CAKE

This is a fast, basic sponge cake that is delicious plain or used in various desserts.

5 eggs, separated
1/4 teaspoon salt
1 cup sugar
1 tablespoon freshly squeezed lemon juice
1 cup all-purpose flour

Beat egg whites and salt until soft peaks form; gradually beat in 1/4 cup of the sugar, beating until stiff. Beat egg yolks with lemon juice until thick and lemon colored; gradually beat in the remaining 3/4 cup sugar. Fold egg whites into yolk mixture. Add flour, 1/3 cup at a time, folding in each part gently. Pour batter into an ungreased 9-inch round spring-form pan. Bake in a 350° oven for 40 minutes or until a toothpick inserted in center comes out clean.
Makes 1 9-inch cake about 2-1/2 inches deep

Note This cake can also be baked in a 10-inch tube pan. Bake as directed.

ZUCCOTTO

A remarkable dome-shaped dolci adorns the Florentine pastry shops. Its outer casing is sponge cake strips steeped in liqueur syrup. Inside are ribboned layers of whipped cream—vanilla, chocolate-walnut or strawberry.

Sponge Cake, preceding

Syrup
1/3 cup each sugar and water
4 tablespoons rum
1 tablespoon Cointreau

Chocolate Filling
1 teaspoon unflavored gelatin
1 tablespoon cold water
2 tablespoons Cointreau
1-1/4 cups heavy cream
1/4 cup powdered sugar
2 ounces semisweet chocolate, grated

Nut Filling
4 ounces semisweet chocolate
1-1/4 cups heavy cream
2 tablespoons rum
1/4 cup chopped walnuts or toasted
   chopped filberts

Topping
1 teaspoon unsweetened powdered cocoa
1 tablespoon powdered sugar

Prepare Sponge Cake as directed in recipe. Cut cooled cake into 3/8-inch-thick vertical slices. Arrange about half the slices in a round-bottomed 2-1/2-quart bowl, placing longest strip in center from rim to rim and each successive shorter slice on either side until inside is completely covered. Patch if needed to fill gaps.

Syrup Combine sugar and water in a saucepan and cook until clear. Stir in the rum and Cointreau. Spoon two-thirds of the syrup over sponge cake lining the bowl. Chill.

Chocolate Filling Soften the gelatin in the cold water; place over hot water and dissolve. Cool; then add Cointreau. Whip cream until soft peaks form and beat in powdered sugar and the liqueur-flavored gelatin. Fold in grated chocolate and spoon mixture into the cake-lined bowl, spreading evenly. Cover with a layer of sponge cake, using about half remaining slices. Sprinkle cake with about half of remaining liqueur-flavored syrup.

Nut Filling Heat chocolate with 1/4 cup of the cream over hot water; stir to blend and let cool. Whip remaining 1 cup cream until soft peaks form and beat in the chocolate cream, beating until stiff. Stir in rum and nuts. Spoon into the bowl, spreading evenly. Cover with remaining cake slices and sprinkle with remaining liqueur-flavored syrup. Cover with plastic film and chill overnight.

To serve zuccotto, run spatula around edge of bowl. Place a serving platter on top and invert cake. Combine topping ingredients and shake through a sieve onto top of zuccotto. Cut into wedges to serve.

Makes 12 servings

Tortes, Cakes & Cookies

BLUE RIBBON SPONGE CAKE

This feathery light sponge cake is excellent plain or frosted.

1-1/4 cups cake flour
1-1/2 cups sugar
1/2 teaspoon each salt and baking powder
6 eggs, separated
1/2 teaspoon cream of tartar
1/4 cup orange juice
1 teaspoon vanilla extract
1 tablespoon grated orange peel

In a bowl sift together the cake flour, 1 cup of the sugar, salt and baking powder. Beat egg whites and cream of tartar in a large mixing bowl until soft peaks form and gradually beat in remaining 1/2 cup sugar; beat until stiff. Make a well in the center of the dry ingredients and add the egg yolks, orange juice, vanilla extract and orange peel. Beat at medium speed for 1 minute. Fold one-fourth of the egg white mixture into batter to lighten it. Then fold in remaining whites. Turn into an ungreased 10-inch tube pan. Bake in a 325° oven for 50 to 55 minutes or until a toothpick inserted comes out clean. Turn upside down to cool, then remove from pan.
Makes 12 to 14 servings

WHITE SHEET CAKE

Surplus egg whites come in handy for this moist light cake. It is a good choice to bake for a children's holiday party as the large frosted surface is easily adorned with colored sugar in the design of a Valentine heart, Easter egg or Christmas tree.

3/4 cup butter
1-1/2 cups sugar
3 cups cake flour
3 teaspoons baking powder
1/2 teaspoon salt
3/4 cup milk
1 teaspoon vanilla extract
1/2 teaspoon almond extract
6 egg whites
Chocolate Sour Cream Frosting, following

Beat butter until creamy and then beat in sugar, beating until light. Stir together flour, baking powder and salt and blend dry ingredients into creamed mixture alternately with milk. Add vanilla and almond extracts. Beat egg whites until stiff but not dry and fold in. Turn into a buttered and floured 9- by 13-inch baking pan. Bake in a 350° oven for 40 to 45 minutes or until the center springs back when touched lightly. Let cool on a rack, then frost with Chocolate Sour Cream Frosting.
Makes about 2 dozen servings

Chocolate Sour Cream Frosting Melt 6 ounces (1 cup) semisweet chocolate bits in the top of a double boiler over hot water. Stir in 1/2 cup sour cream. Spread over cake while frosting is still slightly warm.

FEATHER-LIGHT ANGEL CAKE

Here is an extra-large angel cake, an ideal solution for utilizing leftover egg whites.

1-2/3 cups egg whites (approximately 14)
1-1/2 teaspoons cream of tartar
3/4 teaspoon salt
2 teaspoons vanilla extract
1 cup each granulated and powdered sugar
1 cup cake flour

Beat egg whites until foamy and beat in cream of tartar and salt. Continue to beat until stiff peaks form. Beat in vanilla extract. Sift together sugars and flour and fold into beaten whites. Pour into an ungreased 10-inch tube pan and bake in a 350° oven for 45 to 50 minutes or until a toothpick inserted comes out clean.
Makes 1 large cake, about 16 to 18 servings

CHOCOLATE ANGEL CAKE

This cocoa-flavored angel cake is a pleasant composite of lightness and richness.

1-2/3 cups egg whites (approximately 14)
1-1/2 teaspoons cream of tartar
1/2 teaspoon salt
4 teaspoons water
2 cups sugar
1-1/2 teaspoons vanilla extract
1 cup all-purpose flour
6 tablespoons unsweetened powdered cocoa

Beat egg whites until frothy and beat in cream of tartar, salt and water. Beat until soft peaks form and beat in 1-1/4 cups of the sugar and the vanilla extract. Stir together the flour, remaining 3/4 cup sugar and the cocoa; add to whites and fold in. Turn into an ungreased 10-inch tube pan. Bake in a 400° oven for 10 minutes; reduce heat to 375° and bake 30 minutes longer or until a toothpick inserted comes out clean. Let cool upside down. To serve, remove from pan and slice in wedges.
Makes about 14 servings

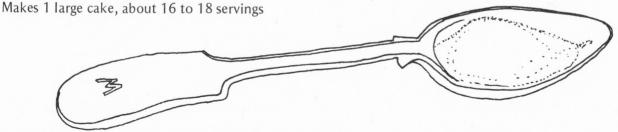

Tortes, Cakes & Cookies

POWDERED SUGAR POUND CAKE

Either bake this fine-textured butter cake in a decorative bundt pan or use small individual loaf pans instead.

3/4 pound butter
1 1-pound package powdered sugar
6 eggs
2 teaspoons vanilla extract
1/2 teaspoon each salt and ground nutmeg
2-3/4 cups cake or all-purpose flour
1/2 cup slivered or sliced almonds

Beat butter until creamy and beat in sugar. Add eggs one at a time and beat until smooth. Mix in vanilla extract, salt and nutmeg. Gradually add flour, beating until smooth. Coat a buttered 10-inch bundt pan with almonds and pour in batter. Bake in a 300° oven for 1-1/2 hours or until a toothpick inserted comes out clean. Or, bake in 4 3-1/2- by 7-inch prepared loaf pans for 70 minutes. Let cool a few minutes on a rack, then unmold from pan.
Makes 1 large cake or 4 small loaves

GOLD LAYER CAKE

A bounty of egg yolks is needed for these golden cake layers. Fill them with a raspberry jelly or apricot jam and dust the top with powdered sugar or turn them into the spectacular Boston Cream Pie that follows.

2 cups cake flour
2 teaspoons baking powder
1/4 teaspoon salt
1/4 pound butter or margarine
1 cup sugar
4 egg yolks
1 teaspoon vanilla extract
2/3 cup milk

Sift together the flour, baking powder and salt. Beat butter and sugar until creamy and beat in egg yolks and vanilla extract. Add dry ingredients to creamed mixture alternately with milk, beating until smooth. Turn into 2 buttered and floured 9-inch cake pans and bake in a 375° oven for 25 minutes or until the top springs back when lightly touched. Let cool on racks 10 minutes, then turn out of pans.
Makes 2 layers

BOSTON CREAM PIE

A custard filling seals together cake layers and a shiny chocolate glaze swirls on top.

1 recipe Gold Layer Cake, preceding
2 cups milk
1/3 cup cornstarch
1/4 cup sugar
1/4 teaspoon salt
3 egg yolks
1 teaspoon vanilla extract
2 teaspoons rum (optional)
Chocolate Frosting, following

Prepare Gold Layer Cake as directed in recipe and set aside to cool. For the custard filling, mix 1/3 cup of the milk with the cornstarch to make a paste. In a saucepan combine remaining milk with sugar and salt and heat to scalding. Blend in the cornstarch paste and cook until thickened. Beat egg yolks until blended, pour in one-fourth of the milk mixture, stir well to blend and return all to pan. Cook, stirring until thickened. Remove from heat and stir in vanilla extract and rum, if desired. Let cool. Then spread filling on one cooled cake layer and top with other layer. Top with warm Chocolate Frosting, making swirls. Let cool and chill, covered.
Makes 12 servings

Chocolate Frosting In a saucepan combine 1/2 cup sugar, 1-1/2 tablespoons cornstarch, 1 ounce unsweetened chocolate and 1/2 cup boiling water. Cook, stirring, until thickened and smoothly blended. Remove from heat and stir in 1 tablespoon butter and 1/2 teaspoon vanilla extract.

WIND CAKE

This is a remarkable cake; foolproof and sturdy, yet light. It is superb plain or topped with berries and whipped cream.

5 eggs, separated
3/4 cup cool water
1-1/2 cups sugar
2 cups cake flour
1 teaspoon vanilla extract
1/8 teaspoon each salt and cream of tartar

Beat egg yolks until light; add water and beat 5 minutes. Add sugar gradually, beating well. Fold in flour and vanilla extract. Beat egg whites until foamy; add salt and cream of tartar and beat until stiff but not dry. Fold into yolk mixture. Turn into an ungreased 10-inch tube pan. Bake in a 300° oven for 1 hour. Turn upside down to cool. Remove from pan when cold.
Makes 12 servings

Tortes, Cakes & Cookies

ORANGE PECAN CAKE

A sleek chocolate glaze encases this fragrant, moist nut cake. It travels well on a picnic outing or in a bag lunch.

6 eggs, separated
1 cup sugar
1-3/4 cups ground pecans
1/2 cup all-purpose flour
1 teaspoon baking powder
1/4 teaspoon salt
2 teaspoons grated orange peel
1/3 cup butter, melted
6 ounces (1 cup) semisweet chocolate bits
2 tablespoons butter

Beat egg whites until soft peaks form and gradually add 1/4 cup of the sugar, beating until stiff and glossy. Set aside. Beat egg yolks until thick and yellow and beat in remaining sugar. Stir together the nuts, flour, baking powder, salt and orange peel and mix into the yolks. Stir in melted butter and fold in whites. Pour into a buttered 9-inch spring-form pan. Bake in a 350° oven for 40 minutes or until a toothpick inserted in center comes out clean. Let cool on rack, then remove from pan. Melt chocolate and butter in a small pan over hot water, stir to blend, and spread over top and sides of cake. Chill to set.
Makes 8 to 10 servings

RAVANI

From the Greek cuisine comes this tantalizing melding of flavors: orange, rum and walnuts in a cake to cut in diamonds.

2-1/2 cups shelled walnuts
10 pieces zweiback
1-1/2 teaspoons baking powder
1 tablespoon grated orange peel
8 eggs, separated
1/4 teaspoon each salt and cream of tartar
1 cup sugar
1/4 pound butter, melted
Rum Syrup, following

Place walnuts and zweiback pieces in a blender in small batches and blend until ground. Turn mixture into a bowl and mix in baking powder and orange peel. Beat egg whites until foamy, add salt and cream of tartar and beat until soft peaks form. Add 1/4 cup sugar; beat until stiff. Beat yolks until thick and pale; beat in remaining sugar. Fold nut mixture into yolks and mix in cooled melted butter. Fold in egg whites. Turn into a buttered 9- by 13-inch baking pan and bake in a 350° oven for 30 to 35 minutes or until set. Remove from oven and pour cooled syrup over. Let cool and cut in diamonds.
Makes about 3 dozen pieces

Rum Syrup Combine 1 cup sugar and 1/3 cup water and bring to a boil; cook until clear. Stir in 1/3 cup rum and let cool.

SWEDISH NUT CAKE

A crunchy broiled caramel frosting finishes this feathery light cake.

3/4 cup milk
3 tablespoons butter
5 eggs
1-1/2 cups sugar
1-1/2 teaspoons vanilla extract
1-1/2 cups all-purpose flour
1-1/2 teaspoons baking powder
1/2 teaspoon salt
Caramel or Almond Frosting, following

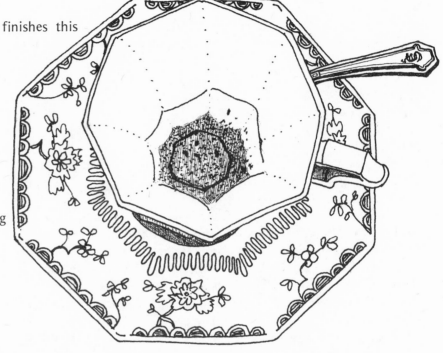

Heat milk and butter until butter melts; set aside. Beat eggs until thick and pale; then add sugar and vanilla extract and beat until thick and ivory-colored. Stir together flour, baking powder and salt and combine with egg mixture. Gently stir in hot milk mixture. Pour into a buttered and floured 9-by 13-inch baking pan and bake in a 350° oven for 30 minutes or until the top springs back when touched lightly. Spread top with Caramel or Almond Frosting and place under broiler until bubbly, about 1 minute. Let cool.
Makes 15 to 18 servings

Caramel Frosting In a saucepan combine 4 tablespoons butter, 3 tablespoons heavy cream and 1 cup firmly packed brown sugar. Heat until mixture begins to bubble. Stir in 3/4 cup chopped walnuts, pecans, almonds or shredded coconut.

Almond Frosting In a saucepan stir together 6 tablespoons sugar, 3 tablespoons flour and 2 tablespoons heavy cream. Add 6 tablespoons butter and heat over moderate heat, stirring, until mixture begins to bubble. Add 3/4 cup slivered blanched almonds.

Tortes, Cakes & Cookies

LUNCH BOX DATE BARS

Brown sugar lends a caramel flavor to these chewy date-nut bars.

6 eggs
1-1/2 cups firmly packed brown sugar
1 teaspoon vanilla extract
1-1/2 cups ground graham cracker crumbs
1 teaspoon baking powder
1/2 teaspoon salt
1 cup ground walnuts, pecans or filberts
1-1/3 cups chopped pitted dates

Beat eggs until thick and lemon colored and beat in sugar and vanilla extract. Stir together the cracker crumbs, baking powder and salt and mix in. Add nuts and dates. Turn into a buttered 9- by 13-inch baking pan. Bake at 350° for 30 to 35 minutes or until set. Let cool, then cut in squares.
Makes about 3 dozen

ROCKY ROAD BARS

The marshmallows melt and lend a chewiness to these favorite rich brownie bars.

4 ounces unsweetened chocolate
1/2 pound butter
5 eggs
1-3/4 cups sugar
1-1/2 cups all-purpose flour
dash salt
1 teaspoon each baking powder and vanilla extract
2 cups miniature marshmallows
1 cup chopped walnuts or pecans

Melt chocolate and butter in top of a double boiler; stir to blend and then cool. Beat eggs until thick and lemon colored and beat in sugar. Mix in cooled chocolate and butter. Stir together the flour, salt and baking powder; add to chocolate mixture and blend well. Stir in vanilla extract, marshmallows and nuts. Pour into a buttered 9- by 13-inch baking pan. Bake in a 350° oven for 30 to 35 minutes or until set. Cut into squares.
Makes about 3 dozen

GERMAN ALMOND CRESCENTS

This buttery almond cookie is a perfect accompaniment to berries steeped in wine or a fruit sherbet.

1/2 pound butter
1-1/4 cups sugar
4 hard-cooked egg yolks, sieved
2 eggs, separated
1 teaspoon vanilla extract
1/2 teaspoon almond extract
3 cups all-purpose flour
1/2 cup finely chopped blanched almonds
1 teaspoon ground cinnamon

Beat butter and 3/4 cup of the sugar until creamy. Beat in sieved egg yolk, raw egg yolks and vanilla and almond extracts. Mix in flour. Beat egg whites until soft peaks form; set aside. Mix remaining 1/2 cup sugar with almonds and cinnamon and set aside. To shape cookies, pinch off about 2 tablespoons dough and roll it between the palms of your hands to form a crescent, tapering the ends. Dip cookie in egg white and then in cinnamon-sugar. Place on a buttered baking sheet and bake in a 325° oven for 20 to 25 minutes or until crescents are golden brown.
Makes 4 dozen

FRENCH BUTTER CRISPS

These butter-wafer cookies simply melt in your mouth. Their fragile texture is due to the unique leavening ingredients.

1/2 pound each butter and margarine
1 1-pound package powdered sugar
2 eggs
2 teaspoons vanilla extract
1/2 teaspoon almond extract or ground nutmeg
4 cups all-purpose flour
2 teaspoons each baking soda and cream of tartar

Beat butter and margarine until creamy and beat in sugar, eggs, vanilla extract and almond extract or nutmeg. Stir together flour, soda and cream of tartar and mix in until blended. Shape into 2 long rolls about 1-3/4 inches in diameter on sheets of waxed paper, wrap in waxed paper and chill 2 hours or longer. Slice as thinly as possible and place on lightly buttered baking sheets. Bake in a 350° oven for about 10 minutes or until golden brown on the edges.
Makes 6 or 7 dozen

Tortes, Cakes & Cookies

CHOCOLATE PECAN BARS

Chocolate, pecans and caramel result in a beautiful combination of flavors.

6 egg whites
1 1-pound package brown sugar
2 cups all-purpose flour
1 teaspoon baking powder
1/2 teaspoon almond extract
3 cups chopped pecans or walnuts
4 ounces (2/3 cup) semisweet chocolate bits

Beat egg whites until soft peaks form and beat in brown sugar, beating until stiff and glossy. Mix together flour and baking powder and mix in. Stir in almond extract and nuts. Spread in a buttered 10- by 16-inch baking pan. Bake in a 300° oven for 30 minutes or until golden brown. Scatter chocolate over the top and bake 5 minutes longer, just to melt. Remove from oven and spread chocolate with a spatula. When cool, cut into bars.
Makes about 6 dozen

ALMOND TEA COOKIES

These delectable nut cookies have a buttery flavor and melt-in-your-mouth texture.

1/2 pound butter
1-1/3 cups sugar
1 egg
1/2 teaspoon each vanilla and almond extracts
2 cups all-purpose flour
2 egg whites
1 teaspoon ground cinnamon
1/2 cup sliced almonds

Beat butter and 1 cup of the sugar until creamy. Beat in egg and vanilla and almond extracts. Mix in flour. Pat into a buttered 10- by 16-inch pan. Beat egg whites until soft peaks form and add the remaining 1/3 cup sugar and the cinnamon; beat until stiff and glossy. Spread over dough. Sprinkle with nuts. Bake in a 400° oven for 20 minutes. Cut in squares.
Makes 6 dozen

Breads
Pancakes

Breads & Pancakes

LEMONADE BREAD

A lemon syrup glazes this cake-like bread after baking, lending a refreshing tang.

6 tablespoons butter or margarine
1-1/2 cups sugar
2 eggs
1 tablespoon grated lemon peel
1-1/2 cups all-purpose flour
1 teaspoon baking powder
1/4 teaspoon salt
1/2 cup milk
1/2 cup chopped pecans or walnuts
1/4 cup freshly squeezed lemon juice

Beat butter with 1 cup of the sugar until creamy; beat in eggs one at a time. Mix in lemon peel. Stir together flour, baking powder and salt and blend into creamed mixture alternately with milk. Mix in nuts and turn into a buttered and floured 9- by 5-inch loaf pan. Bake in a 350° oven for 55 minutes or until golden brown and a toothpick inserted in center comes out clean. Remove from the oven and place pan on a rack. Heat remaining 1/2 cup sugar and lemon juice until sugar is dissolved and slowly pour over the entire surface of the bread. Let cool and remove from pan.
Makes 1 loaf

ZUCCHINI LOAF

The shredded zucchini is camouflaged inside this delicious, moist quick bread.

2 eggs
1 cup sugar
1/2 cup safflower oil
1-1/2 cups all-purpose flour
1/2 teaspoon salt
1 teaspoon baking powder
1/2 teaspoon baking soda
1 teaspoon ground cinnamon
1 teaspoon vanilla extract
1 cup finely grated raw zucchini
1 cup chopped walnuts, filberts or pecans

In a mixing bowl beat eggs until light and beat in sugar and oil. Stir together flour, salt, baking powder, soda and cinnamon; add dry ingredients to egg mixture, beating until blended. Mix in vanilla extract, zucchini and nuts. Turn into a buttered and floured 9- by 5-inch loaf pan. Bake in a 350° oven for 1 hour or until a toothpick inserted in center comes out clean.
Makes 1 loaf

Note If desired double the recipe and divide batter into 3 7- by 4-inch loaf pans. Bake in a 350° oven about 40 minutes or until a toothpick inserted in center comes out clean.

ITALIAN CHEESE BREAD

This warm and golden cheese-streaked bread is perfect for picnics with assorted Italian cold meats, garden relishes, seasonal fruits and a jug of Chianti.

1 package active dry yeast
3/4 cup lukewarm water (110° to 115°)
2 tablespoons sugar
3/4 teaspoon salt
approximately 3-1/2 cups all-purpose flour
5 eggs
1/4 pound butter, at room temperature
3/4 cup grated Parmesan cheese
1 cup shredded Swiss or Gruyère cheese

Sprinkle yeast into warm water in a large mixing bowl and let stand until dissolved. Add sugar, salt and 3/4 cup of the flour and beat well. Add 4 eggs, one at a time, and beat until smooth. Beat in butter. Gradually add enough remaining flour to make a soft dough. Turn out onto a floured board and knead until smooth and satiny, about 10 minutes. Place in a bowl, butter top of dough lightly, cover with a kitchen towel and let rise in a warm place until doubled in size, about 1-1/2 hours.

Turn out onto a floured board and knead lightly. Roll out into a 10- by 14-inch rectangle. Beat remaining egg and mix in cheeses. Spread over dough, covering to within 1 inch of the edges. Starting from long side, roll up and join ends to form a tight ring. Place in a buttered 2-quart round baking dish and let rise in a warm place until doubled. Bake in a 350° oven for 40 minutes or until golden and loaf sounds hollow when thumped. Remove from pan. Serve warm or at room temperature.
Makes 1 loaf

BANANA WHOLE-WHEAT BREAD

Whole-wheat flour enhances the flavor of this moist, cake-like banana bread.

1/4 pound butter or margarine
1 cup sugar
2 eggs
1 cup mashed bananas (about 2 large bananas)
1 cup all-purpose flour
1 cup whole-wheat flour
1/2 teaspoon salt
1 teaspoon baking soda
1/3 cup warm water
1/2 cup chopped pecans or walnut meats

Beat butter and sugar until creamy and mix in eggs and mashed bananas. Stir together the flours, salt and soda. Add dry ingredients alternately with the warm water, stirring until smooth. Stir in nuts. Turn into a buttered and floured 9- by 5-inch loaf pan and bake in a 350° oven for 1 hour, or until a toothpick inserted in center comes out clean.
Makes 1 loaf

Breads & Pancakes

VERONA LOAVES

Butter is folded into these lemon-scented round loaves, producing a layered effect when baked.

1 package active dry yeast
1 cup lukewarm water (110° to 115°)
12 tablespoons butter
6 tablespoons sugar
4 eggs
1 tablespoon grated lemon peel
1 teaspoon vanilla extract
3/4 teaspoon salt
approximately 4-1/4 cups all-purpose flour
1 egg white, lightly beaten

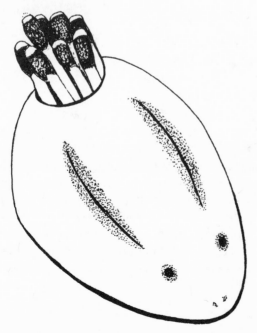

Sprinkle yeast into the water and let stand until dissolved. In a large bowl beat 6 tablespoons of the butter and the sugar until creamy. Add eggs one at a time and beat until smooth. Mix in lemon peel, vanilla and salt. Add yeast mixture and beat until smooth. Gradually add enough of the flour to make a soft dough. Turn out on a floured board and knead until smooth and satiny, about 10 minutes. Place in a bowl, cover with a kitchen towel and let rise in a warm place until doubled in size.

Turn dough out onto a lightly floured board and roll into a 10- by 14-inch rectangle 1/2 inch thick. Cut 3 tablespoons of the remaining butter into small pieces. With narrow side toward you place the 3 tablespoons of butter on the horizontal center 1/3 of the dough. Fold 1/3 of the dough over the butter and place remaining 3 tablespoons butter, cut in pieces, on top. Bring remaining 1/3 of dough over to cover butter. Roll out into an 18-inch-long strip and fold in thirds. Wrap loosely in waxed paper and place in a baking pan. Cover with plastic wrap and refrigerate 20 minutes. Repeat twice, rolling dough into an 18-inch-long strip and folding into thirds, chilling in between.

On a floured board cut dough into 3 pieces. Lightly shape each piece of dough into a ball by stretching the top surface underneath. Place in 3 buttered 8- or 9-inch round baking pans. Cover with a kitchen towel and let rise in a warm place until doubled in size. Brush tops with lightly beaten egg white. Bake in a 350° oven for 30 minutes or until loaves sound hollow when thumped.
Makes 3 loaves

SWISS EGG BREAD

This is a versatile dough that produces beautiful foot-and-a-half-long braids or cinnamon-swirled loaves. It is excellent baked in one- or two-pound coffee cans, as well, strewn with chopped nuts.

2 packages active dry yeast
1/2 cup lukewarm water (110° to 115°)
3/4 cup butter
1/3 cup sugar
1 teaspoon salt
6 eggs
1 cup milk, heated to lukewarm
approximately 6-1/2 cups all-purpose flour
1 egg white, lightly beaten

Sprinkle yeast into warm water and let stand until dissolved. Beat butter and sugar until creamy; mix in salt. Add eggs one at a time and beat until smooth. Add warmed milk and yeast mixture, stirring to combine. Gradually add enough flour to make a soft dough. Turn out on a floured board and knead lightly. Place in a bowl, cover with a kitchen towel and let rise in a warm place until doubled in size.

Turn out on a floured board and knead lightly. Divide into 3 equal pieces for 3 braids. Cut each piece into 3 pieces and roll out each piece between the palms of your hands, making strands about 18 inches long. Place 3 strands parallel on a buttered baking sheet, pinch tops to join and braid as you would a pigtail. Tuck ends under and pinch to seal.

If necessary, place diagonally on the baking pan. Repeat with two remaining thirds. Cover with towel and let rise in a warm place until doubled in size. Brush with slightly beaten egg white. Bake in a 350° oven for 30 minutes or until golden brown. Let cool on a rack.
Makes 3 braids

Cinnamon Loaves Prepare dough as directed above. Let rise in a warm place until doubled, punch down and turn out onto a lightly floured board. Divide dough in half. Roll each piece into a 9- by 12-inch rectangle. Brush with melted butter and sprinkle generously with a mixture of cinnamon and sugar. Roll up from narrow side and place each roll in a buttered 9- by 5-inch loaf pan. Cover and let rise in a warm place until doubled in size. Bake in a 375° oven for 30 to 35 minutes or until loaves sound hollow when thumped. Turn out of pans and let cool on a rack.
Makes 2 loaves

Coffee Can Variation Prepare Swiss Egg Braid dough as directed above, adding 3/4 cup whole or chopped filberts or almonds if desired. Knead and let rise once as directed; then divide dough in half if using a 2-pound coffee can or in quarters if using 1-pound cans. Shape halves or quarters into balls, place in buttered cans, cover with a kitchen towel and let rise in a warm place until doubled in size. Bake at 350° 35 to 40 minutes for 2-pound cans, 30 to 35 for 1-pound cans. Remove from cans and cool. Served sliced in rounds.

171

Breads & Pancakes

CZECHOSLOVAKIAN HOUSKA
(Four-Strand Holiday Braid)

This holiday bread is shaped by braiding four strands of dough to produce an intricate design. Serve hot, thickly sliced and spread with butter.

2 packages active dry yeast
1/2 cup lukewarm water (110° to 115°)
1/4 pound butter
3/4 cup milk
2/3 cup sugar
1 teaspoon salt
5 eggs
2 teaspoons grated lemon peel
1/2 teaspoon ground nutmeg
approximately 6 cups all-purpose flour
1/2 cup chopped almonds
1 egg white, lightly beaten
Orange Frosting, following (optional)

Sprinkle yeast into lukewarm water and let stand until dissolved. Heat butter and milk until butter melts and pour into a mixing bowl. Add sugar and salt and cool to lukewarm. Mix in eggs, lemon peel, nutmeg and yeast mixture. Gradually add flour, adding enough to make a stiff dough. Mix in almonds. Turn out on a floured board and knead until smooth and satiny, about 10 minutes. Place in a bowl, cover with a kitchen towel and let rise in a warm place until doubled in size.

Turn out onto a board and knead lightly. Divide in half; then divide each piece into 4 equal portions. Roll each to form a strand about 21 inches long. Place 4 of the strands diagonally on a buttered baking sheet. Pinch together at one end and braid loosely by picking up the strand on the right, bring it over the next one, under the third and over the fourth. Repeat, always starting with the rope on the right until braid is complete. Tuck ends under and pinch to seal. Repeat process with remaining 4 strands. Cover with towel and let rise until doubled in size. Bake in a 350° oven for 30 to 35 minutes or until golden brown and loaves sound hollow when thumped. Let cool on a rack, then spread with Orange Frosting, if desired.
Makes 2 large braids

Orange Frosting In a mixing bowl place 2 cups powdered sugar and 2 tablespoons orange juice concentrate (undiluted, but thawed) and beat until blended. Add enough water (1 or 2 teaspoons) to make frosting of spreading consistency.

KULICH

This tall and stately Russian Easter bread is created by baking the egg-rich dough in a coffee can. In this unusual mixing method, the egg yolks and whites are beaten separately for a tender pound cake-like result.

2 packages active dry yeast
1/2 cup lukewarm water (110° to 115°)
6 eggs, separated
3/4 cup sugar
3/4 cup milk, heated to lukewarm
1 teaspoon salt
approximately 5-1/2 cups all-purpose flour
2 teaspoons grated lemon peel
1 teaspoon vanilla extract
3/4 cup butter, at room temperature
1/3 cup chopped almonds
Powdered Sugar Glaze, following

Sprinkle yeast into warm water and let stand until dissolved. Beat egg yolks until thick and light and beat in 1/2 cup of the sugar, milk, salt and 1-1/2 cups of the flour. Beat hard until smooth. Mix in lemon peel, vanilla extract and the dissolved yeast, beating until smooth. Cover with a kitchen towel and place in a warm spot to rise for about 1 hour. Mix butter into the raised batter. Beat egg whites until stiff, beat in remaining 1/4 cup sugar and fold egg whites into raised batter. Gradually add remaining flour, working in enough to make a soft dough. Mix in almonds. Turn out onto a floured board and knead lightly. Cover with a kitchen towel and let rise in a warm place until doubled.

Punch down and turn out onto a floured board. Divide into 4 pieces and shape each into a ball. Place in buttered 1-pound coffee cans. Make a foil collar to extend each can 2 inches. Cover with towel and let rise in a warm place until doubled in size. Bake in a 350° oven for 40 minutes or until loaves sound hollow when thumped. Remove from pans and let cool on racks. Make Powdered Sugar Glaze and spread the top of each loaf with it, letting glaze drizzle down the sides.
Makes 4 loaves

Powdered Sugar Glaze Beat 2 cups powdered sugar with 2 tablespoons milk and 1 teaspoon vanilla extract; beat until smooth.

Breads & Pancakes

ITALIAN BREAD DOVES

The egg-rich Italian Easter bread offers an easy-to-shape, pliable dough. Here it makes four charming doves of peace, well-suited to the Christmas season as well.

1 package active dry yeast
1/4 cup lukewarm water (110° to 115°)
1/4 pound butter
1/2 cup sugar
6 eggs
1 cup milk, heated to lukewarm
2 teaspoons vanilla extract
1/2 teaspoon each salt and ground nutmeg or
    grated lemon peel
approximately 6 cups all-purpose flour
Almond Paste Topping, following
 whole blanched almonds
1 egg white

Sprinkle yeast into warm water and let stand until dissolved. Beat butter and sugar until creamy and beat in eggs and milk. Mix in vanilla extract, salt, nutmeg or lemon peel and dissolved yeast. Gradually add flour, adding enough to make a soft dough. Turn out on a floured board and knead until satiny and no longer sticky, about 10 minutes. Place in a bowl, cover with a kitchen towel and let rise in a warm place until doubled in size.

Punch down and turn out on a lightly floured board. Knead lightly, then cut into 4 equal portions. Cut each piece in half and roll out 1 piece into an oval about 3-1/2 by 8 inches for the wings; place on a buttered baking sheet. Roll out remaining piece into a triangle about 3-1/2 inches at the base and 8 inches high. Place like a cross over the wings, with center of triangle over center of oval. Holding the triangle at the center, twist the base of the triangle over once, stretch out and press down to make the tail. Take the top of the triangle and twist it in the opposite direction to form the neck and head. Pull out beak (tip of triangle) with fingers. Repeat this process, making 3 more doves with remaining dough.

Make the Almond Paste Topping and spread over wings and tail. Place an almond in each head for an eye and 4 or 5 almonds at the base of each tail. Cover with towel and let rise in a warm place until doubled in size. Beat the egg white until frothy and brush over entire surface. Bake in a 350° oven for 30 minutes or until golden brown. Makes 4 bread doves

Almond Paste Topping Beat together 2/3 cup of canned almond paste, 2 egg whites and 1/4 cup sugar, beating until blended.

PANETTONE MILANESE

A glaze of almond paste caps this fragrant fruit- and nut-filled bread.

1 package active dry yeast
1/4 cup lukewarm water (110° to 115°)
1/4 pound butter
1/2 cup sugar
3 eggs
4 cups all-purpose flour
3/4 cup milk, heated to lukewarm
1/2 teaspoon salt
1 teaspoon each vanilla extract, grated lemon
   peel and pulverized aniseed
1/3 cup each golden raisins and pine nuts
double recipe Almond Paste Topping, preceding

Sprinkle yeast into warm water and let stand until dissolved. Beat butter until creamy and beat in the sugar. Add eggs one at a time and beat until smooth. Add 1 cup of the flour and beat well. Mix in dissolved yeast, milk, salt, vanilla, lemon peel and aniseed. Gradually add remaining flour, beating until smooth. Mix in raisins and pine nuts. Turn out on a lightly floured board and knead until smooth and no longer sticky, about 10 minutes. Place in a bowl, cover with a kitchen towel and let rise until doubled in size.

Turn out and divide into 3 pieces. Shape each piece into a round and place in a buttered 9-inch cake pan. Make the Almond Paste Topping and spread on loaves. Cover with towel and let rise until doubled in size. Bake in a 350° oven for 30 minutes or until golden brown and loaves sound hollow when thumped. Let cool on racks.
Makes 3 loaves

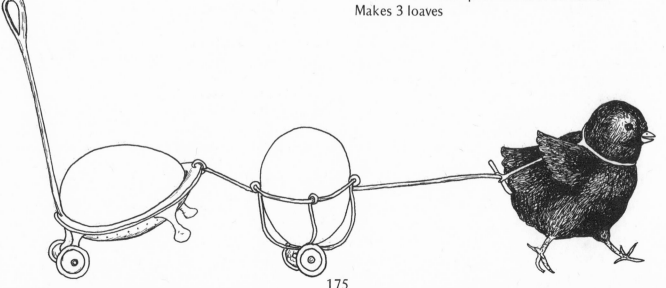

Breads & Pancakes

SLAVIC ALMOND BREAD

Almond paste swirls within this crescent-shaped coffee ring. It is a lovely bread for brunch, accompanying omelets and fresh strawberries with sour cream.

1 package active dry yeast
1/4 cup lukewarm water (110° to 115°)
1/4 pound butter
6 tablespoons sugar
1/2 teaspoon salt
1 teaspoon vanilla extract
1/2 teaspoon almond extract
3 eggs
3-1/2 cups all-purpose flour
2/3 cup milk, heated to lukewarm
Almond Paste Filling, following
1 egg white, lightly beaten
1/3 cup sliced almonds
sugar

Sprinkle yeast into warm water and let stand until dissolved. Beat butter until creamy and beat in sugar, salt, vanilla and almond extracts and eggs, beating until smooth. Add 1 cup of the flour and beat well. Add yeast mixture and milk and beat until smooth. Gradually add remaining flour, beating until smooth with a heavy-duty electric mixer or a wooden spoon. Turn out onto a floured board and knead until smooth and satiny, about 10 minutes. Place in a bowl, cover with a kitchen towel and let rise in a warm place until doubled in size.

Turn out onto a lightly floured board and knead lightly. Cut dough in half. Roll half into a 16-inch circle. Make Almond Paste Filling and spread one half of filling on dough. Roll up and bring the ends together to form a circle. Place in a buttered 9-inch round pan. Repeat with remaining dough. Cover with a towel and let rise in a warm place until doubled in size. Brush with lightly beaten egg white, sprinkle with almonds and sugar and bake in a 350° oven for 35 minutes or until golden brown and bread sounds hollow when thumped. Remove from pans and let cool on racks. To serve, wrap loaves in foil and reheat.
Makes 2 loaves

Almond Paste Filling Combine 1 8-ounce can almond paste, 4 tablespoons butter at room temperature, 2 tablespoons sugar and 1 egg. Beat until smoothly blended.

ITALIAN ALMOND WREATHS

An almond paste glaze bakes on these egg-rich bread wreaths. They are festive loaves to make in quantity, bedeck with ribbons and pass out to friends and neighbors from a wicker basket at the holiday season.

2 packages active dry yeast
1/2 cup lukewarm water (110° to 115°)
3/4 cup each butter and sugar
4 eggs
2 egg yolks
1 teaspoon each salt and grated lemon peel
2 teaspoons vanilla extract
1 cup milk, heated to lukewarm
approximately 6-1/2 cups all-purpose flour
Almond Paste Topping, page 174
1/4 cup sliced almonds

Sprinkle yeast into warm water and let stand until dissolved. Beat butter and sugar until creamy. Beat in eggs, egg yolks, salt, lemon peel, vanilla extract and milk. Stir in dissolved yeast. Add 2 cups of the flour and beat well. Add 1 more cup flour and beat for 5 minutes. Gradually beat in remaining flour with a heavy duty mixer or wooden spoon. Turn out on a lightly floured board and knead until smooth. Place in a bowl and butter top of dough lightly. Cover with a kitchen towel and let rise until doubled in size, about 1-1/2 to 2 hours.

Turn out on a floured board and knead lightly. Divide in 6 pieces. Shape each into a ball, poke a hole in the center, then stretch and shape into a ring 6 inches in diameter. Place on a buttered baking sheet and spread with Almond Paste Topping. Let rise uncovered until doubled in size. Sprinkle with almonds. Bake in a 350° oven for 30 minutes or until golden.
Makes 6 wreaths

Breads & Pancakes

SALLY LUNN

This golden batter bread eliminates the kneading process. Serve warm, in the baking dish if you like, cut in thick slices.

1 package active dry yeast
1/2 cup lukewarm water (110° to 115°)
1/2 cup milk, heated to lukewarm
6 tablespoons butter, at room temperature
2 tablespoons sugar
1 teaspoon salt
3 cups all-purpose flour
3 eggs
1 tablespoon heavy cream

Sprinkle yeast into warm water in a mixing bowl and let stand until dissolved. Add milk, butter, sugar, salt and 1 cup of the flour and beat until smooth. Add eggs one at a time and beat well. Gradually add remaining flour, beating thoroughly. Cover with a kitchen towel and let rise in a warm place until doubled in size. Stir down with a wooden spoon. Spoon into a buttered 2-quart round baking dish, such as a soufflé dish. Let rise again until doubled in size. Brush with cream. Bake in a 350° oven for 35 to 40 minutes or until loaf sounds hollow when thumped.
Makes 1 loaf

CINNAMON SWIRL COFFEE CAKE

A cinnamon-pecan layer ribbons the middle and coats the top of this light coffee cake.

1/2 pound butter or margarine
1-1/4 cups sugar
2 eggs
1 cup plain yogurt
1 teaspoon vanilla extract
2 cups all-purpose flour
1-1/2 teaspoons baking powder
1/2 teaspoon baking soda
1/4 teaspoon salt
3/4 cup finely chopped pecans
1 teaspoon ground cinnamon
2 tablespoons sugar

Beat butter and sugar until creamy and mix in eggs, yogurt and vanilla extract. Stir together the flour, baking powder, soda and salt and mix in, blending well. Spoon half the batter into a buttered and floured 9-inch tube pan. Combine nuts, cinnamon and sugar and sprinkle half of the mixture over the batter. Spoon in remaining batter and top with remaining nut mixture. Bake in a 350° oven for 45 to 50 minutes or until a toothpick inserted in center comes out clean. Let cool on a rack 10 minutes, then remove from pan.
Makes 12 servings

KUGELHOPF

This decorative fluted coffee cake graces the bakeries in Alsace, Germany and Austria. It is a batter-type of yeast bread, so it requires no kneading.

1 package active dry yeast
1/4 cup lukewarm water (110° to 115°)
1/3 cup currants
2 tablespoons sherry
1/4 pound butter
1/3 cup sugar
1/2 teaspoon salt
1 egg
2 egg yolks
1 teaspoon grated lemon peel
1/2 cup milk
2 cups all-purpose flour
whole blanched almonds
powdered sugar

Sprinkle yeast into warm water and let stand until dissolved. Plump currants in sherry. Beat butter until creamy and beat in sugar, salt, egg and egg yolks. Add lemon peel and milk. Blend in yeast mixture and 1 cup of the flour; beat until smooth. Add remaining flour and beat well, about 5 minutes. Stir in currants and any remaining wine.

Butter a deep 9-inch tube pan, preferably one with a fluted design, and arrange almonds in the bottom. Spoon in batter, cover with a kitchen towel and let rise in a warm spot until tripled in size. Bake in a 350° oven for 40 minutes or until a toothpick inserted comes out clean. Turn out on a rack to cool. Dust with powdered sugar.
Serves 12

Breads & Pancakes

CHOCOLATE STREUSEL COFFEE SPIRAL

This is a decorative, fragrant bread. When sliced, the chocolate streusel makes pinwheel patterns.

dough for Slavic Almond Bread, page 176
3/4 cup sugar
1/3 cup all-purpose flour
3 tablespoons butter
2 teaspoons unsweetened powdered cocoa
3/4 teaspoon ground cinnamon
Glaze, following

Prepare the dough for Slavic Almond Bread as directed in the recipe. After the first rising of the dough, turn out dough on a floured board and knead lightly. Divide in half and roll each piece into a rectangle about 24 inches long and 8 inches wide. Make a streusel by combining the sugar, flour, butter, cocoa and cinnamon; sprinkle half of the streusel over each rectangle. Roll up each piece like a jelly roll from a long side and pinch ends to seal. Holding one end of dough, twist it a dozen times to make a rope. Form into a spiral or flat coil and place in a buttered 9-inch round pan. Repeat this process with remaining half of the dough. Cover loaves with a kitchen towel and let rise in a warm place until doubled in size. Bake in a 350° oven for 30 to 35 minutes or until golden brown and loaves sound hollow when thumped. Remove from pans and let cool on racks. Make Glaze and drizzle it on loaves while they are still warm.
Makes 2 loaves

Glaze Combine 1 cup powdered sugar, 1/2 teaspoon vanilla extract and 1 tablespoon lightly beaten egg white.

ORANGE-GLAZED ROLLS

Marmalade swirls within these tantalizing rolls.

1 package active dry yeast
1/4 cup lukewarm water (110° to 115°)
4 tablespoons butter
1/3 cup sugar
1/2 teaspoon salt
3 eggs
approximately 3-3/4 cups all-purpose flour
3/4 cup milk, heated to lukewarm
3 tablespoons melted butter
2 tablespoons light corn syrup
6 tablespoons orange marmalade

Sprinkle yeast into lukewarm water and let stand until dissolved. Beat the 4 tablespoons butter until creamy and beat in sugar, salt, eggs and 1 cup of the flour. Stir in milk and the yeast mixture. Gradually add remaining flour, adding enough to make a soft dough. Turn out onto a floured board and knead until smooth and satiny, about 10 minutes. Place in a bowl, cover with a kitchen towel and let rise in a warm place until doubled in size.

Place 1 tablespoon each melted butter, corn syrup and marmalade in each of 2 9-inch square baking pans. Punch down dough and turn out onto a floured board. Knead lightly. Roll into a large rectangle and spread with remaining melted butter and orange marmalade. Roll up from the long side like a jelly roll and cut in 3/4-inch-thick slices. Place in baking pans. Cover with towel and let rise in a warm place until doubled. Bake in a 350° oven for 35 to 40 minutes or until golden brown. Turn out upside down from pans and serve warm.
Makes about 18 large rolls

GOUGÈRE HAM PUFFS

Golden balls of choux paste flecked with ham and cheese make a savory hot bread to accompany a salad luncheon.

5 tablespoons butter
1 cup milk
1/2 teaspoon salt
1/4 teaspoon dry mustard
1 cup all-purpose flour
4 eggs
3/4 cup chopped cooked ham
1 cup shredded Gruyère or Samsoe cheese
1/4 cup slivered blanched almonds

Heat butter and milk in a saucepan; add salt and mustard and bring to a full rolling boil. Add flour all at once and beat constantly with a wooden spoon over medium heat until mixture leaves the sides of the pan and forms a ball. Remove from heat and beat in eggs one at a time, beating until smooth. Beat in the ham and cheese. Drop from a tablespoon into small mounds 2 inches apart on a buttered baking sheet. Sprinkle with almonds. Bake in a 375° oven for 25 to 30 minutes or until golden brown.
Makes about 2 dozen puffs

Breads & Pancakes

POPOVERS

These can be mixed quickly in a blender.

2 eggs
1 cup milk
1 cup all-purpose flour
1 tablespoon safflower oil or melted butter
1/2 teaspoon salt
2 teaspoons sugar

Place eggs, milk, flour, oil or butter, salt and sugar in a blender and blend just until smooth. Pour batter into very well-buttered baking cups or an iron muffin pan, filling each cup half full. Bake in a preheated 400° oven for 40 minutes or until puffed and golden brown.
Makes 10 to 12 popovers

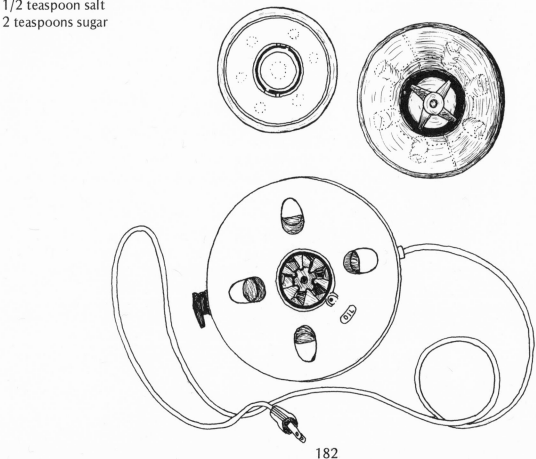

FRENCH TOAST

Choose a rich egg bread as the basis for these crusty brown toasts.

3 eggs
1-1/2 cups milk
1/2 teaspoon vanilla extract
1/4 teaspoon ground nutmeg
8 slices rich egg bread (Swiss Egg Bread, Coffee
   Can Variation, page 171, or purchased)
butter as needed
maple syrup, or
powdered sugar and sweetened, crushed
   strawberries or berry preserves

Beat eggs well and blend in milk, vanilla extract and nutmeg. Dip bread slices in custard mixture, coating both sides. Melt 1 or 2 tablespoons butter in a large frying pan and sauté slices in batches until golden brown on both sides, adding more butter as needed. Top with maple syrup or dust with powdered sugar and serve with crushed berries or preserves.
Makes 4 servings

WAFFLES

These crispy, tender waffles are a treat topped with sweetened sliced strawberries and sour cream or yogurt.

1 cup all-purpose flour
1 teaspoon baking powder
1/2 teaspoon salt
1 tablespoon sugar
2 eggs, separated
1 cup milk
2 tablespoons butter, melted

Stir together flour, baking powder, salt and sugar in a bowl. In another bowl beat the egg yolks and mix in the milk and melted butter. Stir in the flour mixture just until moistened. Do not beat. Beat egg whites until they hold firm peaks and fold into the batter. Spoon batter into a preheated waffle iron. Bake until golden brown and crispy.
Makes 4 or 5 large waffles

Breads & Pancakes

SOUFFLÉ PANCAKES

These large souffléed pancakes are a charming brunch entrée with little grilled sausages alongside. Serve them with berries and whipped cream or Honey Butter, following.

6 eggs, separated
3/4 cup all-purpose flour
1/2 teaspoon each baking powder and salt
1 pint half-and-half
3 tablespoons butter

Beat egg yolks until thick and pale. Stir together the flour, baking powder and salt and mix in. Stir in cream. Beat egg whites until stiff but not dry and fold in. Melt part of the butter in a large frying pan over medium-high heat and spoon batter into pan, making an 8-inch cake. Fry on both sides until golden brown. Repeat with remaining batter.
Makes 6 servings

FINNISH PANCAKES
(Pannukakku)

The billowy oven-baked Finnish pancake makes an excellent brunch dish to embellish with strawberries and sour cream.

4 tablespoons butter
2 eggs
2 tablespoons honey
1/4 teaspoon salt
1-1/4 cups milk
1/2 cup all-purpose flour
powdered sugar, or
berries, sour cream and brown sugar

Melt 2 tablespoons of the butter in a 9-inch round baking dish in a 425° oven. Meanwhile beat eggs with honey, salt and milk. Melt remaining 2 tablespoons butter and add with flour to egg mixture, blending until smooth. Pour batter into the hot dish and bake at 425° for 20 to 25 minutes or until puffed and golden brown. Cut in wedges and serve hot dusted with powdered sugar. Or accompany with bowls of berries, sour cream and brown sugar for topping.
Makes 3 to 4 servings

GERMAN PANCAKES

Dust this pancake with powdered sugar or spread with Honey Butter and roll it like a long thin cigar.

3 eggs
1/2 cup half-and-half or milk
2 tablespoons flour
dash salt
butter as needed
powdered sugar or Honey Butter, following

In a blender container place the eggs, half-and-half or milk, flour and salt; blend just until smooth. Or place in a bowl and beat with a whisk. Heat a 9- or 10-inch frying pan over medium-high heat and butter pan lightly. Pour in just enough batter to coat the pan, tilting pan as you do so. Cook slowly until lightly browned. Turn pancake over and brown other side. Dust with powdered sugar or spread with Honey Butter and roll up tightly. Place on a platter and keep warm. Repeat with remaining batter, adding butter as needed.
Makes 3 to 4 pancakes

Honey Butter With an electric mixer beat 4 tablespoons butter until creamy. Add 1/4 cup honey and beat until light. Gradually beat in 1/4 cup heavy cream and beat until fluffy.

SWEDISH RICE CAKES

Rice is the only thickening in these custard-like pancakes. They are excellent for brunch topped with strawberry preserves. Or drizzle them with Honey Butter (preceding) as a dinner accompaniment to ham or pork chops.

1/3 cup uncooked, long-grain white rice
2 cups milk
dash salt
1 tablespoon honey
3 eggs
dash ground nutmeg

Combine rice, milk, salt and honey in the top of a double boiler. Cover and cook over hot water, stirring occasionally, for 1-1/2 to 2 hours or until milk is absorbed and rice is creamy. Let cool. Beat eggs and mix in nutmeg and the rice mixture. Heat a griddle over medium heat and lightly coat with butter. Drop spoonfuls of batter onto griddle and cook slowly until golden brown on both sides.
Makes about 20 3-inch pancakes

Index

Index

Index

Index

LOU SEIBERT PAPPAS is the food editor of the Peninsula Times Tribune in Palo Alto, California, and the author of a dozen other cookbooks. A former food consultant for Sunset Magazine, she now writes for Gourmet and Cuisine magazines. Her other cookbooks include International Fish Cookery and Entertaining in the Light Style (both 101 Productions) and Vegetable Cookery (HP Books), winner of R. T. French Tastemaker Award for the best soft-cover specialty cookbook of 1982.

MARION SEAWELL is a painter and free-lance illustrator. She has studied at the California School of Fine Arts (now the San Francisco Art Institute) and with Stuart Davis at the New School for Social Research in New York.